Sisters

Sisters

COMING OF AGE & LIVING DANGEROUSLY

IN THE WILD COPPER RIVER VALLEY

by Aileen & Samme Gallaher

EPICENTER PRESS
Alaska Book Adventures ™
www.EpicenterPress.com

Epicenter Press is a regional press founded in Alaska whose interests include but are not limited to the arts, history, environment, and diverse cultures and lifestyles of the Pacific Northwest and high latitudes. We seek both the traditional and innovative in publishing nonfiction books, and contemporary art and photography gift books.

Publisher: Kent Sturgis
Acquisition Editor: Lael Morgan
Editor: Sherrill Carlson
Cover and Book Design: Victoria Sturgis
Mapmaker: Marge Mueller, Grey Mouse Graphics
Proofreader: Susan Ohrberg
Printer: Transcontinental Printing

Library of Congress Control Number: 2004104106

ISBN: 0-9745014-2-5

Booksellers: This title is available from major wholesalers. Retail discounts are available from our trade distributor, Graphic Arts Center Publishing Co., PO Box 10306, Portland, OR 97210. Visit www.GACPC.com.

PRINTED IN CANADA

10 9 8 7 6 5 4 3 2 1

To order single copies of SISTERS, mail $14.95 plus $4.95 for shipping (WA residents add $1.30 state sales tax) to: Epicenter Press, PO Box 82368, Kenmore, WA 98028.

Discover exciting ALASKA BOOK ADVENTURES! Visit our online Alaska bookstore at www.EpicenterPress.com, or call our 24-hour, toll-free hotline at 800-950-6663. Visit our online gallery for Alaskan artist Jon Van Zyle at www.JonVanZyle.com.

DEDICATION

To Robert King for urging me to write,
and to Geri and Earle Mankey for their loving help.

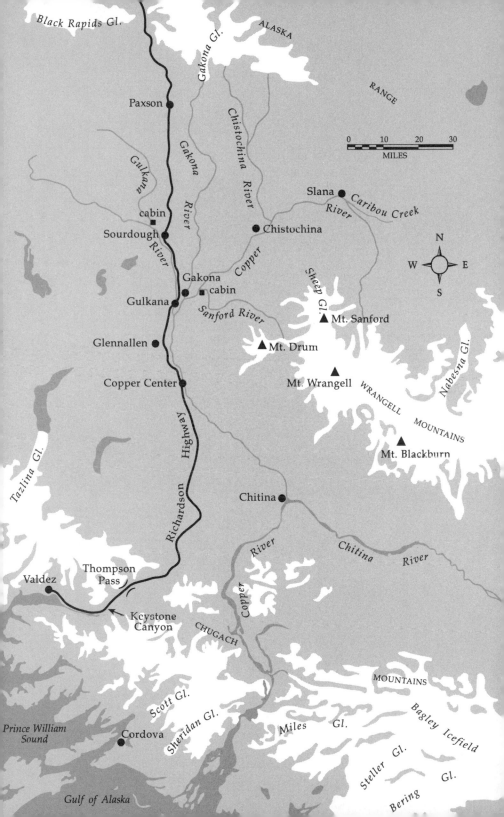

TABLE OF CONTENTS

Aileen, Slim, Samme in Valdez, summer 1928

FOREWORD

This book is the charming history of two sisters from Fresno, California, Aileen and Samme Gallaher, in the Copper River Valley of early twentieth century Alaska. Detailing their adventures with Aileen's gold rush era husband, "Slim" Williams, it provides a rare understanding of what it was like to live in the Copper River Valley not so many years ago when forces that continue to shape the region today — including cars, airplanes, and tourists — were being felt for the first time.

This was a period of special personal change and growth for the two sisters as they came to know and love this unique region. Samme's retelling of this unforgettable period, supplemented by Aileen's writings before her death, provides a delightful account of the colorful people and events they knew and witnessed. It is also a moving story of the forces that would bring an end to their charmed life in the wilds.

While the Copper River Valley had been inhabited for ten thousand years or more by Native people, changes brought by Western culture were initially slow to arrive here. In the 1920s and 1930s, the time span of this book, many of the older ways of surviving in this challenging environment were still in force. Most Native people continued directly living off the rich resources of the land and rivers. They inhabited fish camps in the summer months, and then camps elsewhere in the valley in other seasons to harvest moose, trap, pick berries, or hunker down for the long winter's cold. Some even remembered when the first white U.S. government exploration party called Allen Expedition (Alaska's "Lewis and Clark" Expedition) passed through the region in 1885.

∞

With the discovery of gold in the interior of Alaska in the later nineteenth century, more Westerners would come, increasingly so with the breaking of a trail from the deepwater port of Valdez into the heart of Alaska (now the Richardson Highway) in 1898. By the early 1900s, roadhouses had been established along the route, providing supplies, lodging, and meals for the earliest travelers, and, later, gasoline for those with the first cars who attempted the daunting trip over a still rough, but improving, road.

The result was increasing and then sustained contacts with Westerners, altering the lives of Native people at a rapid pace. By the 1920s some of their ancient patterns were changing because of the new cash economy emerging in the Copper River Valley and also strict requirements that they educate their children in government schools. On the other hand, many of the white settlers in the region were adopting some of the traditional Native ways of life, including travel by dog team, hunting, and trapping. Slim Williams, Aileen's then middle-aged husband, was one of many adventure seekers who came up for the gold rush in their youth but then settled in to live off the land. It was this lifestyle, especially having dogs for transportation, that would so charm his young wife and his sister-in-law, Samme. The Gallahers' unusual, first-person account provides much needed understanding of what life was really like in this area at this time in Alaska's history.

∞

My direct involvement with this fascinating story began in the summer of 2000. I was told by co-workers at the Bureau of Land Management that a sister-in-law of Slim Williams was traveling to Gakona in the Copper River Valley, about fifteen miles north of Glennallen, Alaska.

Would I be interested to meet her? The answer was a quick "yes."

In 1987, as an archaeologist and historian, I had investigated the remains of one of Slim Williams' trapping cabins in what is now the Sourdough Creek Campground in the Copper River Valley, about thirty miles north of Glennallen. I had also learned a little about the man from Ahtna Elders near Gakona, and later met a few others who had known Williams before his death in 1974 at age ninety-three.

What I discovered was intriguing. Williams was a character whose real life filled with numerous adventures had been blurred with exaggerated stories, some of which he told himself. So, with the opportunity to meet his sister-in-law in 2000, I was excited with the prospects of learning more. I assumed she was a sister to the woman Williams married after he left Alaska, *the only wife I knew he had.* Instead, I soon discovered that Samme's sister Aileen had been with him in Alaska for several years and that as a teenager Samme had lived with them in 1927–28 and again in 1930-31. The stories she told about their adventures were absolutely fascinating, and she recalled them with clarity and rich details, as if they had occurred only yesterday. Her comments gave me such personalized insights into how life was really lived in the Copper River Valley that I encouraged her to write a book!

What you will now read is a most remarkable story by a most remarkable person. My only regret is that you all cannot meet Samme in person and become her friend as I have been so privileged.

Robert E. King Ph.D.
State Archaeologist
U.S. Bureau of Land Management
Anchorage, Alaska

View of Mount Wrangell from the Richardson Trail

PROLOGUE

It rained all night, but now it has stopped and the clouds are gone. Across the valley, I can see Mount Sanford shining brightly in the morning sun. It has not changed one bit from the first time I saw it, seventy-four years ago. I was a bright and eager fifteen-year-old, and unlike the mountain, I have changed quite a bit. There are the mountains that we loved – Mount Drum, Mount Wrangell, and Mount Sanford – keeping watch over the Copper River Valley. They are as beautiful as ever, and as I sit here gazing at their splendor, the nostalgia is almost overwhelming. I can almost hear the sounds of those years I lived here – the noise a team of huskies makes dragging a loaded sled – the squeak of the sled runners on packed snow – the driver talking to the dogs, urging them on. But most of all, I feel the presence of my sister, Aileen, who lived six years here in the Copper River Valley wilderness of Alaska.

It all takes me back over the years to the day when we waved a tearful goodbye to her as the train pulled out for Seattle. Aileen was on her way to Alaska.

Samme Gallaher Darnall
Chistochina, Alaska
July 2001

PART I

Aileen Gallaher

1926

THE DECISION

*T*he sudden blast of the ship's whistle startled me. I had been busy getting things in order in my stateroom and I was unprepared for it. I knew it meant that we were about to leave. As the ship began to move, for the first time I felt afraid about the journey I was taking. It had been a huge choice to make, but I had been happy about it. Now, with the sensation of the ship backing away from the dock, I felt a sense of panic. It was too late to turn back, however, and after a few moments of tension, I realized there was no reason to feel afraid. It had taken me a year to decide to make this trip, and I didn't want to turn back now.

I suppose anyone who might have noticed me would have seen a well-dressed young lady, small and petite, who appeared to be quite normal. But I don't believe that I was normal. In fact, I was a runaway. Yes, I was running away from a life that I found intolerable. This journey was a means of escape from the humdrum, day-to-day monotony of my existence. I had dropped out of high school in my hometown of Fresno, California, because of financial difficulties in my family. The only job I could find was with the telephone company as an operator – a "number, please" girl. It was very boring.

My romance during this time was an old school friend, Ike Bailey, who wanted to marry me. I rode the streetcar to work, and it was about a mile walk from my house. Ike worked as an automobile mechanic, finishing his work day at the same time I did. He would meet me after work every day in the same old way, always waiting there as I got off the streetcar. Since he didn't have time to go home and clean up first, he smelled of car grease and had it all over him. It was very unpleasant, and I would have preferred to walk that mile by myself, but he insisted on being there to pick me up. After he took me home, he would go and get all cleaned up and then come back to see me. I liked him, but I did not love him, and I did not want to be married. I longed to find something else, somewhere, that would be exciting and challenging.

In the late summer of 1925 that something appeared, and it turned out to be a tall, charming man from the wilderness of Alaska. He had given a talk at the Odd Fellows Lodge on his life in the North, and my father, Roy Gallaher, had heard him. He was so impressed by this man that he asked the Alaskan to come to our home for Sunday dinner. He accepted the invitation, came to our home, and also impressed the rest of the family.

The man's name was Clyde C. Williams, but his exceptional height had earned him the nickname of "Slim." He was somewhat homely, but he had a beautiful voice. When he smiled and talked, he seemed almost handsome. At forty-four, he was more than twice my age. His face was deeply lined, but his whole appearance was pleasing. His skin was deeply tanned from exposure to the elements, his eyes were bleached brown with flecks of gray, and black hair crowned his striking appearance. He told many interesting stories about his dogs, his log cabin, and life in the woods. Everyone was intrigued. No one was aware, however, that this big man was sweeping me off my twenty-year-old feet.

There was an attraction between us that I felt deeply, and I boldly asked him to come see us again.

He did come back many times, and we found that we really liked each other. It seemed so romantic for him to be interested in me. He was soon to return to Alaska, and he jokingly said one evening, "Why don't you come back with me?" Of course we both laughed at that. Then I said, "I'd love to live there. I'd love the challenge of living in the wilderness." We looked at each other a long time, and the idea for me to actually go to Alaska was born. We talked long into the night, and he was very honest about his description of how life was in Alaska. It did not frighten me, even though it was quite primitive; it seemed very exotic, which only enticed me more. Since I was not yet twenty-one, we thought it would be better for me to wait until the next year. Then, if I still wanted to come, he would send for me.

As the year went by, Slim and I corresponded, and he told me more about his adventures with the dogs and trap line he operated for his livelihood. He always referred to my desire to be in that land. As the months went by, the possibility of my going to Alaska was becoming more real. I was consumed by a desire for something fresh and new, something completely different. Life in Alaska would be much more exciting than my present existence, and I knew this was what I wanted to do. In February of 1926 I turned twenty-one, and in the spring I wrote and told Slim I was ready.

In the meantime, my father had checked on him. He found out that Slim was born in the little village of Piedra in the hills east of Fresno and had relatives living in Fresno. He learned something of his background and found him to be an honorable man. Slim had spent many years in the wilderness of Alaska and had lived a very colorful life. He had prospected for gold, hauled mail, mushed dogs, and trapped for fur. He had been a pioneer in a land with many challenges and few restrictions. Slim had come back to California because his lungs had been frosted during an unforgiving Alaskan winter, and the doctor recommended that he go home to his family in Fresno. He told Slim, "I've known of horses to recover from frozen lungs, but never a man." However, Slim did recover, after he had plowed about five acres of ground in the hot San Joaquin Valley sun for his brother. He claimed that hard work in the sun had healed him. Knowing more about Slim, my parents felt better about permitting me to make the journey.

So here I stood on the deck of the SS ALASKA, on the way to Slim and the "Land of the Midnight Sun." I would leave the ship in Cordova, Alaska, and board the train for Chitina, where Slim would be waiting for me.

I remember the beauty of the Inside Passage as we sailed by islands so close you could almost reach out and touch the trees. The color of the sea, changing when the sun shone on it through scurrying clouds, was delightful. I remember the fun of watching the seagulls as they followed the ship all the way. They would land on the deck rail and squawk, and when you would speak to them, they would turn their heads from side to side. Everything I saw on the trip was new and exciting to me, but as the ship drew closer to Alaska, thoughts of my dear Slim flooded my being.

At last we docked in the quaint little town of Cordova. It was nestled right up against the mountains with little room for a settlement. The main street was unpaved and rather short, with flat-faced buildings on each side, fronted by wooden sidewalks. Many people were there to meet the boat and welcome the newcomers, and everyone was friendly. I had no trouble finding help to move my luggage onto the train. I left for Chitina after only a few hours in Cordova.

I'm sure that the scenery was beautiful, but I don't remember much about it. As I neared the end of my journey, I felt all quivery inside with anticipation. The few remaining hours quickly dwindled to a few minutes – and finally there he was, grinning from ear to ear. As I started down the steps of the train, Slim just stepped up and lifted me down. Then I was in his arms. He held me very close for a few moments. As he let me go, he said, "What took you so long?" We laughed, and I felt more at ease. This big man made me feel safe and wanted, and I knew right down in my heart that if we could laugh at such trifles together, we could make it.

After my luggage was loaded onto a small truck, we started north for the Copper River Valley. The drive from Chitina, with glimpses of the Copper River, was breathtaking. The four towering mountains that hem the valley stood out in the glory of bright sunshine: Mount Blackburn, volcanic Mount Wrangell, beautiful Mount Drum, and Mount Sanford. These glorious sentinels, especially Mount Sanford, were to become a cherished part of my life.

We drove as far as Copper Center that day. There I was introduced to a wonderful lady, Florence "Ma" Barnes, who owned the roadhouse. When I met her, I liked her immediately. She was friendly, unpretentious, and reminded me of my mother. She made me feel welcome, and told me that if I ever needed help, I could come to her. She was looking right at Slim when she said it. His response was just a big grin. Lucy Craig, a young girl just my sister's age, was living with Ma as her ward, and seeing her made me feel a little homesick for my family. That soon passed when I met William Fox, a sad character who was Ma's right-hand man. He was tall and thin, and Ma was growling at him because he had drunk her last bottle of vanilla. That evening Slim, Ma, and I talked late into the night. They exchanged stories, and I listened. I learned that Ma had come from New Zealand to Alaska and bought the Copper Center Roadhouse a few years earlier. After midnight we turned in, and I learned that Alaskans like to talk late into the night, especially in the summertime when it's light and they don't know or much care what time it is. My tiny room was hardly big enough for the cot, but it was comfortable and cozy, and I slept like a newborn puppy.

Copper Center Roadhouse

The next morning I was introduced to the novelty of sourdough pancakes. They all laughed at the amount that I ate. The pancakes, covered with blueberry syrup, were delicious, and I just couldn't stop eating. After Slim almost had to drag me away from the table, we were on our way. Our next stop was Gulkana, where I met Mrs. Griffith, the owner of the roadhouse, her daughter Mary, and Hans Dittman, the handyman. After we left Gulkana we drove up the road to a landing, and Slim showed me a grand view where the Gakona river flows into the Copper River. Our last stop was the Gakona Roadhouse. There I met Arne Sundt and Herb Hyland, who ran the post office and store. They were our closest neighbors, and we would see them often.

At last we were on our way to our wilderness home. About seven miles from Gakona we turned onto a one-way rutted trail, then into a clearing, where we stopped.

Slim said, "This is as far as we go by car; the rest of the way down to the river, we walk." I dug into my carrying case and pulled out a pair of tennis shoes that I had used for strolling the deck of the ship, put them on, and said, "Let's go."

The path down to the steel-gray-colored Copper River was narrow but well worn, so the going was not difficult until it got steep. Slim stopped and turned around to face me, then pulled me into his arms. He held me close for a few moments, and then said, "Stay close behind me. If you feel yourself slipping, just grab me and hold on." In this way we went slowly down to the river.

A big, clumsy looking rowboat was anchored at the bank, with one good oar and another one with a split blade. After we loaded the few things we had brought from the car, Slim lifted me into the boat, jumped in, and cast off into that swiftly moving glacier stream. I wasn't exactly afraid, but I was relieved when we got to the other side, a distance of about three hundred feet. After I got my footing on the rocky beach, I was able to look around, and for the first time I saw where I would live – a log cabin on the banks of the mighty Copper River in the very heart of Alaska.

MY NEW HOME

*A*fter Slim had secured the boat, we started for the cabin, which was about a hundred feet from the moorage. A good feeling came over me as I saw the lovely location of the main cabin, the cache on high pole stilts, and the storage cabin in the back.

Tucked into the woods and riverbank as it was, it had a cozy atmosphere. There was a sense of security and stability about the whole area. I already knew I would love it.

As we approached the yard, the dogs barked, whined, and jumped to greet us. Each dog had its own little log house covered with moss, and a few of them stood on their roofs, and wiggled and jumped.

Copper River cabin

The others strained at the edge of their tethers. Slim spoke very lovingly to each one as he introduced me to Stub, Brindle, Beaver, Sonki, Stik, Blue, and Blizzard. They hardly paid any attention to me, as they were all waiting for a pat from Slim. After he gave his attention and affection to each one, we went to the cabin.

As Slim opened the door for me, I gasped. It was so small I couldn't believe it. But I went in and looked around, and then I saw that it was livable after all. It was neat, clean, and homey. A big cast-iron cooking stove was in the corner by the front door, and beside it was a sturdy-looking worktable. Against the wall was a cupboard for dishes and cooking necessities. The heater in the middle of the room was a fifty-gallon oil drum. It had a big hole cut out of the top with a cover and a stovepipe. Two handmade chairs and a small table completed the furnishings. Small windows on each side of the main room had green and white checked curtains, hung on wires that sagged in the middle. Across the back of the main room was an opening leading into a smaller room, where I could see one bed behind a drawn-back canvas curtain. I looked away, and as I did, there was Slim smiling expectantly at me. He said, "Well, what do you think? It's not much, but it's not mortgaged, and we can fix it up any way you want."

With all the control I could muster, I replied, "This is just fine. As you know, I didn't expect a palace." But my knees almost betrayed me.

As I averted my eyes from Slim, suddenly I couldn't believe what I saw, and I gave a little gasp. Hanging on the wall beside the door was a telephone. It was an ancient oaken hand-cranked monstrosity. I just stared at it for a moment, then asked, "Where did that come from?"

"When I knew you were coming, George and I ran the wire from Gakona. I thought it would be a good idea for you to have it in case of any emergency. And besides that, it's great for getting the latest gossip from down the trail," Slim replied with another big grin.

"Well, it's the last thing I would have expected. How does it work? Is there a central office?" I asked.

"No," Slim said, shaking his head, "you just turn the crank. Two for Gakona, three for Gulkana, a long and two shorts for Copper Center. Our ring is two longs and one short. So if you hear that, just pick up the receiver and talk. If it's any other ring, pick it up anyway and listen – everybody does."

After laughing about the gossip and such, I felt the tension from the long day and the unfamiliar surroundings start to fade away.

Slim had to go back to the car, to bring over the supplies and the rest of my luggage. It would take him a
couple of hours, as he would have to make two trips up
the hill. Off he went, and I was alone.

So this was it, I thought, my new home. I had made
my commitment, and I was determined to keep calm, to
accept things the way they were and never complain;
but as I sat down on one of the little chairs, it wobbled,
and I burst into tears. With Slim gone, I had a good
chance to compose myself. I realized it was just a reaction to all that had taken place that day, so I dried my
tears, stood up, and took it all in. I never cried again
until six years later when I said goodbye to Slim, the
dogs, and Alaska.

When Slim got back, he built a fire in the cookstove,
so we could have some tea. It was refreshing, and I
told him about my wonderful trip. Then Slim stood
up and said, "I'm hungry. Let's have an onion omelet.
We've got some fresh eggs, and we can't get them very
often."

"That's great. I'm hungry too, so what can I do?" I
replied.

Slim grinned at me and said, "Not tonight, Aileen.
I'll cook now and turn it over to you later." After a good
meal of omelets, canned peaches, tea, and cookies, we
were both weary. It had been a long, strange day for
both of us. When it was apparent that I was quite sleepy,
Slim said, "Honey, just go in the other room and get into
your nightclothes, and I will come in later."

After I had changed to my nightgown, I crawled into
bed. Oh, it felt so good to stretch out and relax, and the
next thing I knew, I was awakening to a very bright morn-

ing. Slim was lying beside me sound asleep, so I got out of bed quietly and got dressed.

I went outside to look around and explore my new surroundings. The doghouses were out in the front and off to the left; the river was to the right. A log storage shed stood on the right side of the cabin to the rear, and on the left sat a high cache on stilts. The dogs were beginning to stir, and I longed to go and pet them. But Slim had warned me not to get too close at first, so I just stood there and watched my new world get started on its day.

Before too long I heard Slim moving around, and soon he came out. He put his arms around me and really kissed me for the first time. I felt a little shy about the affection but soon yielded to his caresses. We spent the rest of that day getting things in order, making plans, and laughing about nothing. We were both very happy to be with each other. Every time I would get close to him, Slim would grab me and kiss me. By the end of the day, I was not so shy as I had been. My experience in affairs of the heart was limited, and Slim, knowing my innocence, was very gentle and thoughtful of me. I suppose that I had seen too many Rudolph Valentino movies, for I thought our first night of love would be more romantic. Again, as with the cabin, if that was the way things were, so be it.

When I awoke the next morning, Slim was busy building a fire in that "monster" in the corner – the wood cookstove. He saw that I was getting up and said, "Good morning, Baby Girl. You stay right there. I'll bring you a cup of coffee as soon as it's made." (He followed this custom and brought me coffee every morning in bed for the next six years.) My first taste of that strong coffee

almost brought tears to my eyes. He put a handful of coffee into a pot of water and let it come to a boil, then stirred it to settle the grounds. It was much too strong for me, but I did not want to be a complaining female, so I just gulped a little and said it was good. I was very glad when we got a proper coffee-maker.

Aileen and Slim at Copper River cabin

I drank one cup of coffee, and then I had to get up. I put on my robe and slippers and made my way out to the scourge of the wilderness – the privy. It sat up on a little knoll and it was a "two-holer," although I never needed to share it with anyone. It did not smell like roses blooming in the spring, and a Sears catalog hung on the wall between the holes. I finally did get accustomed to it, but it took some time.

After breakfast we went out to see the dogs. They were to be my dogs too, and I was eager to know them. All of them accepted me with wagging tails, and whines and whimpers of their own. I was thrilled beyond words to be with those wonderful sled dogs. Each was individual and expressive in a unique way. Sonki would toss his head around and act downright silly when you got close to him; I nicknamed him "the clown." Klute was a proper little lady, and would prance around like a little French mistress. Stub acted like a dowdy housewife, and Beaver always liked to fight and stir things up. They all loved to sit on the roofs of their little log houses and watch the activities of the house. If you just said in normal conversation, "Let's go," they recognized those words and starting jumping around, barking and whining to get going.

There were many things for me to learn, and the first one was how to use that "darned" stove. I could make a fire in it, but I couldn't regulate the heat for baking. I needed to make bread, and making the dough was easy. The baking of it was the real challenge. I finally did conquer it by trial and error – many trials and even more errors! Eventually I learned how to bake anything we wanted. However, in the process, I learned a few new cuss words.

Then there was the rifle. It had to be learned and perfected before we could leave the cabin area for hunting and exploring. I had learned to shoot a pistol out on the ranch in California and was good at hitting a bull's-eye, but I had never shot a rifle. The first time I did, I thought I was going deaf, but after a few weeks of practice, I got used to it and was ready to go. Slim gave me a Savage 300 rifle, a "lady's gun," as he called it. It was never off my back whenever we ventured away from home base.

As the days went by, I gradually learned how to live in the wilderness. It was a happy, carefree life, full of the beauty that surrounded us. The Copper River was fascinating to watch – the currents, the color changes with the light, the sounds it made. I grew to love it, and I felt as though it were something of my very own. It ran deep into my heart and remained there all of my life.

HOPPY ARRIVES

*T*hose following weeks were full of excitement and adventure for me. We made many trips into the forest around our cabin to look for signs of game and fur-bearing animals. Our seven-mile jaunts to the post office at Gakona were full of laughter and fun. There were always people to visit on those trips, and, of course, there was the great pleasure of receiving mail from home.

Our nearest neighbor was George Bellefontaine, who was called "the Frenchman." He lived on our side of the Copper, about seven miles up the Sanford River. He had a fox farm up there and raised his own fur-bearing animals in relative isolation, which was required for that kind of operation. When he went to Gakona he came by our place, as the old trail from his fox-farm came right through our yard, and he needed Slim to row him across the river. When he returned he would signal with a couple of rifle shots, and Slim would row over and get him. I soon sensed that George did not like me very much; he was always polite, but he never stayed very long with us. It took me some time, however to realize that he was jealous of me. I had interfered with his relationship with Slim. In the past he could stay over with his old friend and have a good visit. But with me there, it was not the same.

One day George came almost running into our yard, calling Slim. He wanted Slim to go up to his place and help him bring down four wolf pups that he had found. The mother had been shot, and when he had found the pups, he had carried them to his cabin in a gunnysack. So Slim went back up the river with him to help bring down the pups in net-covered crates. Three of the pups were to be sent to Chitina on their way to zoos, and we were to keep one.

A fur trapper needs strong dogs for his team. Slim said that our team needed refreshing, and proper breed stock was a major factor in the process. Acquiring a wolf was very important to us, as we hoped to breed stronger dogs with a wolf as sire, and eliminate the effects of inbreeding.

After they were taken from the crates, we selected one puppy that growled less and with less ferocity. We put a tiny collar with a light chain on his heavily furred neck, and staked him within twenty feet of the cabin door. There I was able to watch him as much as I liked. His fur was a yellowish gray. The most interesting part of him was his eyes, which were bluish gray with yellow spots. His ears stood up as if on alert, and they seemed too big for the rest of him. He kept his tail tightly pulled to his belly. His legs sprawled or doubled up, his paws gripped the earth, and his black nails hooked into anything and everything. My heart ached for him, seeing him try so hard to adjust to this strange place, and a deep attachment to this little wolf took hold of me. When this pup moved about, he kind of hopped, and when the Frenchman returned and watched him, he proclaimed, "His name is Hoppy." It was a most suitable name for this wonderful animal.

At first the pup seemed too young to be dragging around a chain on a neck that was far too small for the rest of him, so in a few days we constructed a pen for him. We used small poles and chicken wire, and covered it with boards. Occasionally we allowed Hoppy to come out and mingle with the dogs. In all his galloping, rolling over, crouching, and joyful playing with them, he never seemed to lose sight of that wire house. When the dogs' play became too rough, he retreated and made a dash for the opening to his pen. The first time he tried to get in, he must have gone a dozen times around the pen to find the gate, which opened away from a corner of the cage. He kept missing it, until he stopped and deliberately turned around and started in the other direction. Then he walked right into its opening. After that, I never saw him lose that direction into his cage again.

Hoppy eventually outgrew his little home, and we decided to put him on a chain. There was a big tree about twenty feet from our front door, which seemed to be a good place for him. Slim made a slip rope around the base of the tree and attached Hoppy to it with an eight-foot chain. This gave the wolf a big circle in which to move. We called it "Hoppy's Circle." If Slim came near,

Hoppy would pull away from him as far as his chain would allow. It was obvious that the wolf did not want to have anything to do with Slim. In order for Slim to handle this wild animal, he had to knock him out. Slim disliked having to do this, but it was the only way that he could change Hoppy's collar.

Gradually I began to get near the wolf and talk to him. Then I put my hand out to him, and with some apprehension at first, he let me pet his head. From then on we were a joy to each other. Now I could watch and pet him as much as I liked. He was my entertainment.

Soon my days were filled with watching Hoppy. It was not too long before he was steady on his legs and spent his days trotting around his circle. His main interest was the dogs. If one of them came close, he would crouch and completely humble himself. To the eight adult sled dogs, he was a curiosity as well as a pup. One old female, Coo, undertook to protect him from another female, Stub, who resented his crawling, whining, and licking subjection. Stub would snap at him and reject his attention. Then Coo would snap at Stub. Here again, I felt this desire to care for and protect Hoppy. It was hard for me to keep my thoughts on anything else but this wolf.

Soon Hoppy was as big as any of the sled dogs. In spite of his size, he was still groveling and whining for attention from them. By this time, I felt that I had become as important to Hoppy as he was to me. He would whine in my direction, and I would always go out and pet him. Those were intimate, loving times for us, but I never attempted to pet him when he was in a playful mood. His moods were very plain. I could tell at once what he wanted – petting or playing —and I only provided the petting.

Aileen and Hoppy. Aileen raised this wild timber wolf.

In the meantime, the fall season came, and in early October I saw my first snowfall. To a city girl from California, the snow was wonderful. I loved every flake of it. With the snow came the serious business of teaching me how to drive a dog team. Slim and I took short trips to instruct me how to handle the sled and direct the dogs. It was not a task – it was just plain fun at first. Then, when we took some longer trips, Slim would have me take the sled. He would trot along behind and would let me recover from my dives into snowbanks, skids on ice, overturns, or my few runaways without his help. He was a demanding teacher, as he knew I would have to mush by myself some day. That graduation day finally came, and for the first time I was to drive the dogteam alone! Nearly two months of hard lessons and narrow escapes had schooled me for this adventure – this day when I would

go alone on the fourteen-mile round trip to Gakona to get
provisions and mail. A freighter had cleared an ice trail
on the Copper River that morning, using a horse-driven
snowplow. He told us that the trail to Gakona was good.

Getting dressed in my winter garments, which were
mostly wool, was a chore. Over my cotton panties and
bra, I struggled into a wool union suit, with a buttoned
flap in the back. Next I put on a wool shirt, and then I
pulled on a pair of men's denim pants. Tucking the shirt
into the pants was a job, because men's pants were not
made to allow for women's hips. My feet were the funni-
est. After two pairs of wool socks, a pair of lambskin
packs, and another pair of cotton socks, I put on
moosehide, Native made moccasins. My normally size
7s were now size 10s. Pulling my parka over all of this
and securing my mittens with a braided wool harness, I
was ready to go.

When I opened the door, the dogs greeted me with
yelps and leaps. They always knew when we were going
someplace. In their excitement, they jumped wildly about
me as I put five sled dogs into their harnesses. In front
was Stub, the leader, followed by Klute, the black Mala-
mute, and Tillie, the Toiler. The wheelers next to the sled
were slow Blue and the sometimes hard-working Sonki.
They were eager to go and were already straining at their
leashes.

So when I released the sled and leaped to my place at
the back and yelled, "Mush," they were off. In a flurry of
snow churned up by the teeth of the brake, we dashed to
the river bar. Across the frozen beach we raced. Dogs
love to make turns, especially sharp ones, and the angle
at which we approached the plowed trail was acute. My

tense hold on the handlebars was almost broken as the sled tipped and twisted after galloping dogs.

Sharp ears pointing to the back, tongues out and tails high, the dogs ran. Stub flashed me a glance over her black shoulder. She almost seemed to be grinning. Chains and metal snaps clinked against creaking wood. Steel sled runners squeaked on bits of snow. Frost from the dogs' breath gathered on their shoulders, and around my cap hung tiny icicles from my own deep breath in the icy cold air.

Dark spruce trees and towering clay banks whirled away from us. I gripped the handlebars and kept my feet steady on the sled runners as I straightened up into the wind whipping by us. There was nothing here of dull city life, only beauty and freshness, frost, scenery, and movement. As I felt the power in the dogs, the feeling of adventure seized me – the excitement and exhilaration of handling a dog team alone for the first time, on a frozen river in the heart of Alaska.

Increasing their speed, the dogs anticipated the cut-off from the river to the trading post. I called, "Gee," and Stub turned so quickly that she almost fell. Then she saw an old Indian trail and started to go that way. I had to call, "Whoa, Stub, haw, into the trail." The dogs got a little tangled up with this fast change, but they straightened out and headed for Gakona.

Soon we charged into the yard of the post. Every dog strained at the harness and wagged or whined in excitement. Standing with all my weight on the sled brake, snow spewing from under my heels, I called for help to get my team into a safe place. We had to get off the main trail, in case another musher came into the area. If teams get together, it could mean a free-for-all dog fight. As any dog musher will tell you, that's not fun.

Herb Hyland came running out to help find a place for me. I followed his direction and stopped the dogs where he pointed. Only when I had that sled securely tied and the dogs quiet, did I relax. Herb walked over to me and didn't even say hello. He looked around and said, "Where's Slim?"

With a big, proud smile, I replied, "He's at home."

Herb shook his head and said, "You drove the dogs down here by yourself?"

"Yes, I did," I replied, "and it was my first time alone with the dogs."

We were walking up to the roadhouse, and as we entered Herb announced, "Attention, everyone. This young lady has just made her first trip alone with a dog team. Let's give her a hand!" There were about five people there, and they all clapped enthusiastically. I felt a little foolish for a moment, and then delighted at being acknowledged. I made a clumsy little curtsy but comically almost toppled over in my heavy parka. Amidst further congratulations, Arne Sundt served drinks all around – hot tea, that is. I couldn't stay long because at that time of the year daylight was short, and I still had to get home before dark. Herb helped me get my supplies and load them onto the sled. The people in the roadhouse all came out and waved me out of the yard. The return home was slower, as the sled was heavily loaded with supplies and the dogs were less eager to go at a breakneck speed. I had time to think about what I had done, and I felt a deep sense of pride. For the first time in my life, I was extremely pleased with myself. My first trip alone had launched my career of driving a dog team, and I loved it!

MY FIRST WINTER

*N*ow that I could drive the team alone, and go into Gakona for mail and supplies, Slim could get on with his work for the coming winter. There were harnesses that had to be mended and kept in working order. Just getting the wood stacked in was a big job. Trees had to be cut, dragged in from the forest by the team, then sawed into stove-length logs and split.

The daylight began to shorten, and the weather began its yearly assault on man and beast. There were days when blizzards raged, and we could hardly get out to the privy. The dogs curled up in their little log houses, and the wolf dug a hole for himself. There were long, lazy days when the wind blew and the snow fell. The temperature dropped daily, getting progressively colder and colder. Sometimes on the coldest days, we'd hear our cabin creak and groan like it was straining to fight off the bitter chill just to keep us warm.

On days during the winter when it was too cold to be out in the sled, we would read and talk about a future trip we dreamed of making to Canada. On one such day, while snuggled cozily inside during a heavy snowstorm, we conceived a new idea – an even longer trip by dog team to the States! We almost gasped as the idea unfolded. We became excited by the magnitude of that trip – by the vastness of the country to be crossed and by the endurance that would be required, both of dogs and of humans. Surely great public interest would be generated in the States and in Alaska, and then there was Canada we'd have to cross. Why, it would be an international thing! It would be the trip of a lifetime. We had no idea where that dream was to lead us, but it was thrilling to think about it.

In the meantime, Hoppy was growing into a huge and beautiful wolf. When he was less than a year old, he was larger than any of the domestic dogs, yet still a pup. He would gambol around the team whenever they were turned loose to be harnessed, or whenever they were turned out of the harness at the end of a trip. He would cringe and roll over, whine and squeak like an un-weaned puppy. Generally, the adult male dogs had no use for him. He was a stranger and an infant, he did not smell right, and he groveled. However, he did get much attention from the younger animals, especially the pups, from the time they could walk until they were a few months old. One of the mother dogs tolerated him from a distance, while another avoided him, but Hoppy loved them all and doted on the pups.

Young wolf pup

Watching this wolf became a constant pastime. His actions and movements were all new to us. When we saw some pups starting toward him for the first time, we stood in tense silence. Our eyes were glued on those toddling, trusting bits of life edging their way into the reach of a wild animal – captive, but still of the wild. He was a beast of the wilderness with a reputation among men that was notorious for slyness, willful destruction, and even crimes of slaughter. He was the animal whose name stood figuratively for the villain in many a play, and gave meaning to the label given to con artists – a "wolf in sheep's clothing." A white pup and a black pup crawled within a nose-length of that huge head and those powerful tusks. Out of that dazzling mouth slid a wide tongue, and those brownish-gray eyes almost closed. The two tiny pups were gathered up into the lonely, loving embrace of tongue, yellow legs, and furry chest. At that moment, we let out a sigh of relief and smiled. A deep love for Hoppy, and for all wolves, began to take hold of me.

Hoppy and I were very good with each other. He seemed to love me especially, and he became a part of my heart. I felt a love for him as I had never felt for any other pet before or since. It was odd, though, that he never cared for Slim. The whole time Hoppy was growing up, he never became tame and loving with Slim, in spite of Slim's attempts at friendliness.

During the previous winter, Slim had run his trap line up the Gakona River. He had left a camp up there with all his needed gear, so he decided to go back this winter to trap. Also, we had been invited to spend Christmas at Chistochina up the river about twenty-five miles on our way to the Gakona trapping area. It took us a few days to pack for the move. After we loaded up, we left in a flurry of snow crystals and headed for Chistochina. It would be my first Christmas in Alaska, and I was eager to go.

We had to take Hoppy, which required quite a bit of extra work on my part. By this time the wolf and I were very compatible; I could easily handle him, but Slim had to keep away from him. After the dogs were in harness, I would unloose Hoppy and attach him with a short chain to the front of the sled. He would run right along beside the wheel dogs and thoroughly enjoy himself. He did annoy the dogs, which couldn't be helped, and he irritated Slim, who clearly resented Hoppy's friendliness toward me. He would have gotten rid of the wolf, but for the fact that we wanted pups from Hoppy. Also, by this time my obsession for Hoppy was intense, so Slim knew that I would not stand for his harming Hoppy in any way.

*Dogs In harness on ice, with Hoppy chained
to the front of the sled.*

The sunset glow of mid-afternoon lighted our arrival in the yard of the Chistochina Roadhouse. Our host, "Red" Hurst, hailed us as we arrived. Several Natives stood about, to see how other dog mushers worked. Forty-three dogs yelped and lunged on their chains as we maneuvered our team alongside a pile of logs. We unhitched our dogs and Hoppy, tied them to the logs, gave them their supper of dried salmon, and left them chewing. We stamped and brushed snow and frost from ourselves, and followed our host into his lodge.

The government had built this log building years ago as a telegraph station. The ground floor consisted of two fifteen-foot rooms with large windows, two outside doors, and a lean-to storeroom in back. The second floor, a half story, held six beds. A partition at one end of this dingy bunkroom formed a tiny bedroom. It was furnished with one window, two chipped iron bedsteads, a dilapidated trunk, a faded packing-box table, and a pale candle. Only the quality and brilliance of woolen blankets, brought fresh from the store, saved the room from complete gloominess.

The lodge guests included two trappers, a fur trader, two Native women, Slim, and me, the only white woman. The two Native women were Belle, the fur trader's wife, and her cousin, Maggie. Curiously, Belle always used both her husband's names – Lawrence DeWitt – whether she was speaking of him or to him.

Like the language of the Eskimo, these Natives' words ran together. I found it difficult to get a sensible translation of any but the simplest expressions. But we all spent the evening exchanging stories and experiences about the trapline and the hunt, and those adventures were the best Christmas Eve entertainment I could imagine.

Christmas Day celebrations began with a barber party. One of the trappers and a Native named Frank Charlie were quite skillful with scissors and razor. Haircuts were exchanged and were presented to those needing them, including Slim.

The dinner feast was "larrupin," a word we used to describe a truly delicious meal. Steam rose from dishes of locally grown boiled potatoes, moose steaks, caribou stew, and dark red beans (which actually tasted better when cooked in the Far North). Our host called the bread he baked "dough gobs." They were huge baking powder biscuits, very light on shortening. Butter, jelly, and syrup were served in their tin containers. My contribution to this feast was a large, four-layered, banana custard-filled cake. We had very carefully carried it on the sled just for the occasion.

I noticed that, of all the diners, Belle and Maggie ate little other than the meat, especially the boiled caribou. Knowing that their daily menus consisted almost solely of caribou, I thought it a poor way to celebrate. The cake garnered no interest from the two girls. As soon as they finished their audible eating, they left the table without a backward glance. Lawrence DeWitt called Belle back to the table to taste the cake. She took a bite of it and pushed it away. Fancy food, which was strange and sweet, did not appeal to her.

After dinner many Natives from the area came to dance and visit throughout the evening. A phonograph supplied the music. The songs "Wreck of the Old 97" and "It Ain't Gonna Rain No More" were the only records played, and those at a screeching pitch. The Natives danced a hop, much like the modern two-step. Their selections of partners seemed strange to me. Men danced with men more often than they danced with women. The women danced with each other. Mr. DeWitt came to me, as I supposed, to ask for a dance. But, no – in a low voice he told me that Belle wanted to dance with me. I assure you that it was a real honor not only to be accepted, but also to be sought out by one of these timid Native women. Belle was one of Chief Nikolai's daughters, and she was honored as such.

After we danced, she asked me to go upstairs with her. In the stuffy room directly above the immense heater on the main floor, she motioned to me to sit beside her on the bed. Her open friendliness puzzled me. From a pocket of her skirt, she drew a small package and handed it to me. I had noticed no exchange of gifts among the Natives, yet here was one of them expressing Christmas in the white man's way, her husband's way.

Finding the spirit of Christmas in this place, so unexpectedly, was very touching. Moved almost to tears, I memorized that scene: log walls, a frosted window, the glowing candle flame, the smiling dusky face, and the gift. The package contained a pair of dainty loop earrings, and I believe she selected them herself. I have kept them among my most treasured souvenirs, and always will remember that special Christmas because of them.

When the "Old 97" had been wrecked seven dozen times, and an ancient clock showed midnight, the party ended. Belle, Maggie, and I went upstairs to the small bedroom. Unlike them, I removed more than my moccasins. They snickered openly at my masculine underclothing, which was a pair of woolen long johns. I crawled into the single bed and left the candle for them to put out. In the darkness I listened to their giggling, audible gum chewing, and strange sibilant language.

Then the sounds of the "silent" Northern night began. River ice, tightening in the increasing cold, popped and groaned. A spruce tree snapped with the frost in its heart. A dog rattled his chain, and an owl mocked his own famous question. In the far distance, wolves began their song of the wild.

I snuggled down and fell asleep, thinking how different Christmas was at home, three thousand miles away.

THE TRAP LINE

*T*he day after the Christmas celebration, December 26, 1926, we headed out for the Gakona River and the trap line. It was tough going up the Chistochina River. Slim broke trail on snowshoes, and I followed with the team and Hoppy. A heavy load was hard on the dogs and the sled handler, so we didn't make good time. We spent two nights huddled in a tent set deep in the snow for insulation. Wrapped in our heavy Hudson's Bay blankets, we kept warm. We arrived at the base camp in the afternoon of the third day, with just enough daylight to get settled before dark. We were very tired after that difficult trip, but after a couple of days taking it easy and putting the camp in order, we were ready to go again.

Aileen with ax at trap line camp

After a day or so arranging his trapping gear, Slim left to set out his trap line. I wasn't going out with him yet, as he didn't want to take time instructing me. That could come later, so Hoppy and I stayed alone. This was most welcome to me, as I could write to Mother and just enjoy this wonderful land. Whenever the dogs were gone, Hoppy missed them, crying for them to return. Since I was quietly occupied, he was lonely and began to howl softly outside.

All alone, I sat and listened to that lonely cry. Perched on the bedding of a crude bunk, my world was filled with the "call of the wild" as I looked about me. The walls of the olive drab tent crowded close to a hand-hewed table, a bunk made of small logs, a mattress of spruce needles, Hudson's Bay blankets, and an airtight heater. Firewood was stacked behind the stove. Under the table was boxed grub – beans, flour, sugar, dried fruits – and magazines, guns, axes, dog harnesses, and rope. The tent was warm and cozy, and the caribou stew was beginning to boil, filling the air with its delicious aroma. I could sit comfortably on the bunk and stir the steaming caribou hocks, while the subzero atmosphere pressed at the twelve-ounce canvas.

The squeak of a step on hard-packed snow caused me to listen. Then came the soft, "moo-oo-oo" of the wolf again. I stretched and stood up. I was dressed in my usual wool clothing and Native-made moccasins. I found that I was beginning to enjoy my clothes that at first had seemed bulky. After stirring the stew again, I opened the flap of the tent. The wolf fell silent as I stepped out of the tent into glittering daylight. After the ticking of the Big Ben, the crackling of spruce fire, and the bubbling of stew, the "great alone" seemed breathlessly still.

I faced the south, and through a hundred miles of frost air I gazed at the three sentinels of the Copper River Valley. Volcanic Mt. Wrangell wore a white plume of steam above a spread-eagle cloak of ice; Mt. Drum seemed to crash into the sky with craggy serrated peaks; Mt. Sanford soared to a glistening arched dome. I looked to the low hills in the west that flanked the Gakona River, on whose bank I stood. An expanse of ice, snow, and piles of driftwood stretched for a mile to a stand of dark timber, and shimmered in the golden light of the low January sun. Warm springwater caused a heavy mist to hang along the trend of the riverbed. A lake in the distance glittered and shone like a musical saw. Then, as I gazed at a black, bushy promontory three miles downriver, my ears became attuned to the world of my eyes. A tree cracked under the pressure of severe cold, and a raven cried "allah-allah" as he flew over, heading downriver to a remote roost. A mink showed his head and shoulders not ten feet away, studying me as I sat perfectly still. Then he rustled across an opening into a different hole. Two chickadees tweeted on a spruce branch close by, flitting, gossiping, and flirting.

Then I heard the whisper of feet on snow again, and the lonely whine of a canine. I turned about, and there stood Hoppy looking straight at me. Poor dear, he wanted company. As I moved toward him, he waved his tail and leaned my way. In five steps I was beside him. He turned his back that I might stroke him, and lifted his head for me to scratch under his collar. He always welcomed me, the one who scratched, petted, and talked to him. The big dogs were generally indifferent to the wolf, but I gave him the attention and affection he seemed to need. With Hoppy there, I never felt lonely.

I stayed in camp alone that first week while Slim organized his trap line. During those days in that little tent, with the snow piled high around it, I was able to think about myself. Why did I love this so much? Maybe it was because there were no worries – no bills or rent to pay – just Mother Nature and Father Elements. Back home in California, I had been so fastidious about everything that if someone used my hand towel, I'd growl about it. But here, even our crude bathing equipment didn't bother me in the least. I was a changed person, and I liked my Alaskan self better.

In her letters to me, my Mother worried that I would miss the movies, which I had always loved. I told her that I could step outside any time and get a whole show just by speaking. Stub would dance, Beaver would wiggle, and Sonki would shake hands by sprawling his big paw above his ear. Blizzard would just sit and look at the others, being so beautiful that he didn't have to do anything, and Klutina (we called her Klute) could talk by the hour. And, of course, there was always Hoppy to watch. So you see, I did not miss entertainment. I was contented with this devil-may-care life. It suited me, and I suited it. Slim called me a brick, a regular "pardner," and a baby girl. He was a great person to live with, always cheerful and ready to laugh. He never complained about anything and only cussed at the dogs. They understood the language.

The day after the traps were set out, a terrific wind started to blow. It didn't let up for three days. It was a time for reading and dreaming. We decided that it was best not to go to Canada as we had planned. We would make more money trapping, and we could take the trip later. Anyhow, if we went, what would we dream about when the weather kept us inside?

One morning after a hearty breakfast of bannock, bacon and beans, we started out to break a trail down to a creek that Slim had spotted from high ground. After a few miles of traveling, the snow got deep, and we plowed into strange territory along the creek. We were winding in acute angles and horseshoe curves with snow up to our knees, and Slim was breaking trail without snowshoes. We expected at any moment to arrive at the mouth of the creek emptying into the Gakona River, but it was getting later and later and we were still not there. At three o'clock Slim took an observation from a high point but could not see the Gakona River.

We thought of turning back, but we had come quite a distance. The creek had to end someplace, and we expected to find it soon. On we plodded, but still there was no sign of the river. It was cloudy, and before long darkness began to shadow the creek. All eight of us were extremely tired. After a short stop, I could not get the dogs to budge, and Slim had to walk back and coax them out of their slump.

Finally, while it was still light enough, we sighted a cabin. It proved to be a cabin that Slim had seen before, but no one would have wanted to stay there overnight.

Sadly, a man had blown his brains out in there, and it had never been cleaned up. So on we went. Slim now had a good idea as to our location, and we soon found another cabin near a sawmill. We jimmied the padlock and entered the building. A coal oil lamp served us well, but a large Yukon stove did nothing but smoke. We poked around and found the rusted shell of an old heater to make a fire in. It felt great, although we were lucky that it was not very cold, no more than ten below zero.

We had no ropes or chains with which to tie the dogs outside, so for once, they slept inside. We had to watch them closely to keep them from getting scorched against the stove. It did happen once with Blue's tail, and the burnt hair nearly asphyxiated me. Slim didn't mind very much. I tried to lie down by a couple of dogs for warmth, but they just thought I was playing, and would hop up and wag their big old tails. So I had to give up and join Slim on a table with our parkas for pillows and covers. I went right to sleep, and didn't wake up until morning.

All we found in the way of food for breakfast was some coffee beans. There was no coffee grinder, so we just melted some snow and boiled the beans in an old rusty pan. Such coffee — ugh! I like mine lightly tinted with cream, nice and mild. But I drank a cup of the bitter brew nonetheless before we left. It helped to get me moving.

Slim knew where we were now, so we made our way to the river, perhaps a couple of miles. Slim was breaking trail and I was handling the sled. His job was tougher, but manning the sled was a rough job, too. At one point I got dizzy and lightheaded from hunger, but I had to keep going. We were a very happy and hungry bunch when we finally pulled into our home camp. Hoppy was overjoyed at our return, whining and running back and forth trying to find someone for affection. As tired as I was, I went over and petted him.

"Well, really, it isn't what a person *can* do, it is what they *will* do," Slim observed. He added, "There are lots of men who would have needed to be hauled into camp, or who would have given up in some way at the first inconvenience or hunger pangs, so I'm really proud of you and your courage."

Quitting had never entered my mind. It seemed natural just to go on following my "pardner," since he was usually working at least as hard as I was, or harder. I appreciated his words of praise.

Our six wonderful dogs also needed praise. They were noble little fellows – Blue, Beaver, Sonki, Klutina, Blizzard, and Stub. They covered trap line, hauled wood, freighted supplies, moved fur, and managed to do all the work required of them.

When our trapping season ended in February, it was time to head for home. We loaded up the sled with our pelts, harnessed up the dogs and Hoppy, put out the fire, and yelled, "mush." It took us four days to get to our Copper River cabin.

It was good to be home and just relax. Slim went down to Gakona three days later for the mail. The news from home was exciting because my parents had decided to allow my youngest sister, Samme, who was fifteen years old, to come and stay with us for a year. She would be coming up in July, and we had to rearrange the cabin for her.

We took some time to go down to Gulkana and Copper Center and visit our friends, and I had all the leisure I wanted to watch my wolf.

We also had a constant visitor and talkative neighbor for several days. A great gray wolf came out of the timber and sat on the bar, a short distance away. He watched the camp and then went into the brush, out of sight, and howled and howled some lonesome tale. Maybe he wanted to help Hoppy. The stranger followed the same pattern for many days, and then we never saw him again. The whole incident gave me a sad, lonely feeling that took days to shake off, yet it deepened my sense of awe at these magnificent wild creatures.

We knew Hoppy would probably be around 165 pounds when he was grown. He was already some beauty. I patted him and scratched him, and he thought it quite a joke for me to take his front feet and lift him to a standing position, where he was taller than I. He was scared of Slim and would not play when he was near, but kept his eyes on every movement Slim made. That disturbed Slim. Although he said nothing about it, I could tell that he was unhappy about the situation.

As the season began to change, the sun crawled higher into the sky and there was something new to see every day. The birds were so beautiful to watch, and the songs of chickadees and camp robbers filled the air. I never heard any real silence. There was always a bird chirping or hooting, a restless dog, a soft breeze in the spruce, the fire crackling or roaring, and more frequently, the river popping as it tried to free itself from its icy straitjacket. It reported like the crack of a .30-30 rifle. The ice humped into a mound, then

Valdez, Alaska

Valdez from the water

blew out like a tire, sending out loose chunks the size of a large book. It sounded as if we were being bombarded. The sunrises and sunsets were like none I had ever seen before. The beautiful mountains were always there, and the sun would shine on them through the moving clouds, constantly changing the scene with their shadows. Of course, the northern lights were a great source of delight, impossible to describe fully. Some nights we could even hear them pop and crackle across the sky in splendid sheets of pulsating color. Sometimes I just sat and thought, and it seemed some greater power was trying to show me these sights.

The rest of the spring went by, and the days got longer. In May the ice in the Copper River "went out." We heard the great roar first, and then the whole body of ice moving at once. It was spectacular beyond imagination or description.

The ship carrying Samme would soon be arriving in Valdez. Anticipation of the trip to Valdez filled our thoughts, for this would also be our wedding day. We had been happy for one year together, so we had decided to make it permanent. On July 16, 1927, at three o'clock in the morning, the *SS Alaska* docked in Valdez, and my little sister walked down the gangplank and into my arms.

Later that day Slim and I were married in a dear little church in Valdez, with my sister as maid of honor. I was now Mrs. Clyde C. Williams, and was called Mrs. Slim, for short.

PART II

Samme Gallaher

1927

SAMME'S STORY

*W*as I really going to Alaska? I could hardly believe it, but the little green ticket I held in my hand indicated that it was true. Aileen and Slim had sent it for the *SS Alaska,* which would leave Seattle on July 10, 1927. It would arrive in Valdez on July 16, carrying me as a passenger, and Slim and Aileen would be on the dock in Valdez to meet me.

Aileen and Mama had made all the arrangements, and I did very little to help, just whatever Mama told me to do. I knew I wanted to go, but it would be a whole year away from my dear mother. Every time I thought about that, I would start to cry. It would also put me a year behind in school, but I didn't cry about that. School had never been my first choice of places to be. The adventure of the com-

Samme at Gakona, Alaska, 1928

ing journey, and a life in Alaska with Aileen and all her dogs, appealed to me. Aileen was my very special sister. She was seven years older than I and had always mothered and babied me. We were alike in many ways, and I wanted to share her interesting life.

Some of my friends had a departure party for me the evening before I left. All of those good wishes and goodbyes made me realize that I would truly be leaving the next day! I became so excited about the trip that I could barely sleep a wink that night.

The next morning Mama, my sister Una, and I set out on the eight-hundred-mile drive from Fresno, California, to the dock in Seattle. The four-day trip was like a vacation for all of us, and it helped me make the transition between home and the real beginning of my journey northward. When we finally arrived in Seattle, they accompanied me safely on board the ship, and Mama turned me over to the care of the stewardess. I knew it was hard for her to let me go. We all went to my stateroom and tried to be cheerful, but when the "all ashore" sounded, and they were leaving the ship, tears began to flow. They stood on the dock, and watched and waved for a long time until I was out of sight. That was a sad moment for me, so I rushed to my stateroom where I could really bawl in private, but then I got a lovely surprise. There on my bunk was a bouquet of flowers and a box of chocolates from Mama and Una. I didn't know how they got them there, but I was delighted and stopped crying.

The first night at dinner, the menu was new to me. Since I didn't know how to order from it, I asked the waiter for some spaghetti. He was amused, I knew, but very obliging, so I got the spaghetti. Later my roommate, Therza Rossman, a young schoolteacher from Trail, BC, Canada, showed me how to order, so I did not have to eat spaghetti all the way to Alaska.

Sailing up the Inside Passage was the most enchanting experience a young girl could ever expect to have. On the second day, the crew informed us that we would be sailing past the city of Prince Rupert at midnight, so Therza and I decided to stay up to see it. As midnight approached, we began to see lights, but they were bobbing up and down and moving. We could not imagine how all that motion could come from city lights. As we got closer, we saw that they were not city lights, but a huge fishing fleet. Our ship slowed to quarter speed as we approached the boats, and it took us two hours to get through the vessels. We learned that they were gillnet boats, out to fish a large salmon run. We never did see Prince Rupert.

After brief stops at many little picturesque coastal towns and a journey of six days, the SS Alaska arrived in Valdez at three o'clock in the morning. As it docked, we could barely see the pier due to a thick fog. The few people who were on the dock could be seen but not recognized. However, I did make out two people waving, and as they came closer to the ship, I could see that it was Aileen and Slim. I was thrilled to see them, and when the gangplank was lowered, I ran right down it into Aileen's arms. We clung to each other and laughed and cried. Then Slim said, "Leave some for me." We laughed at that, and after Slim got his hugs, we walked the few blocks to the Golden North Hotel.

It was so early in the morning that we all needed to get back to bed. Aileen and I went to our hotel room, but we had trouble falling asleep. First we would think of one thing to say, and then we would think of one more. Finally, however, even though our joy at seeing each other again was exhilarating, sleep came at last.

We awoke to a bright sunny day. The fog had lifted, and I was eager to see Valdez. When I stepped out the front door, I almost fell over backward as I looked up at the mountains surrounding the town. They towered right out of the ocean, leaving little space for Valdez. Even in July they were covered with snow. The little town was alive and busy. The few blocks that I could see had several two-story buildings on each side of the street. All the buildings lined up together facing on a wooden sidewalk. What a pretty, little "movie set" town, I thought.

This was a special day for Aileen and Slim. It was their wedding day. We walked to a beautiful little Episcopal church, where they were married. There were four guests besides me, and I was the bridesmaid. After kisses and congratulations, a hearty Alaskan breakfast completed the celebration. That was the first time I had ever been to a wedding, and I thought maybe I would like to do the same thing someday. Not for a long time, though, as I was only fifteen.

We spent the rest of the morning shopping for the items I would need for my new life in the woods. Aileen and Slim bought me high-top Keds, a pair of Levi's, a woolen shirt, a man's felt hat, and a .22-caliber rifle. Slim told me that I needed to learn on this smaller gun, which was good for shooting birds. Later, I would learn to use a .30-30 rifle for shooting larger game. It was exciting to shop for all of that new stuff, and Slim and Aileen had as much fun as I did. Then they purchased other supplies,

Samme and Lucy Craig at Copper Center

loaded the car, and before long we started for the Copper River Valley.

The gravel and dirt road from Valdez followed the Lowe River, and at Bridal Veil Falls it abruptly started up a steep mountain. For several miles it wound high along the canyon wall, hewn from solid rock. It was too narrow to allow two cars to pass, so if they met, the one coming downhill had to back up to a wider space. We did meet a car close to the top, and they had to back up a short way so we could pass.

From various places we could see the canyon floor and the river directly below us, and at Snow Slide Gulch men were working to build a bridge. They said an avalanche took the bridge out every year. They had placed two very large planks across the gulch for us. Slim would not drive over them, but Aileen would. The men had her line up our wheels with those planks, and she drove right across. That was the scariest part of the trip. I was very relieved when we got out of the mountains and down onto a safer road. I had been to Yosemite a number of times over the top of the high Sierra Nevada Mountains, but that road was nothing to compare with this one through the Keystone Canyon and over Thompson Pass.

Our first stop was Copper Center, about one hundred and twenty miles north of Valdez. There I met Ma Barnes. Aileen had written many good things about her, so I felt as though I already knew her. Lucy Craig, a girl my age, lived there as Ma Barnes' ward. We had our dinner at the roadhouse, and it was certainly a new experience for me. The big table was set for twelve, which was all it would hold. There was no menu, and everyone ate whatever had been cooked, just like at home. That night it was beef stew, or maybe caribou, I didn't ask. As we ate, other diners came in and sat down at any open space at the table. Everyone seemed to know everyone else, and the conversation was lively. I really enjoyed seeing those Alaskans eating, talking, and trying to tell the best story. I thought, what a great way to enjoy dinner.

Lucy and I were the only teenagers in that part of Alaska, and we became good friends for the rest of the summer. She was soon to go "outside" to a school in Oregon, which would leave me as the only teenager living in the wilderness of the Copper River Valley. If there were any teenagers, they were sent to Valdez or Fairbanks for their education, as there was no school system in that part of the territory at that time.

Our next stop was Gakona, about thirty miles north of Copper Center. The Gakona Roadhouse there was a huge log building, which really could not be called a cabin. It had a second story and a high-pitched roof. The Gakona River flowed swiftly about fifty feet in front of it. The lobby was a large room without any decoration and only a few wooden benches for furniture. In one corner, a staircase led to the bedrooms upstairs, and the other corner was occupied by the Post Office. Across the front next to the lobby were the dining room and the kitchen, and behind were the owners' quarters. The two men who lived there and operated Gakona Roadhouse were Arne Sundt from Norway and Herb Hyland, from Sweden. Both welcomed me warmly to Alaska, and made me feel at home in this new, amazing world.

After picking up mail and registering Aileen's new name, we drove about seven miles up a dirt road, and turned off into the woods to park the car in a clearing.

Keystone Canyon on the Richardson Highway, east of Valdez

This completed our motor trip. We walked down to the boat, and each of us took as much as we could carry. Aileen told me that Slim had made a new path, and it was not so steep as it was when she first came.

The trip across the river scared me almost as much as the mountain trip. At the place where we crossed, the river narrowed and was very swift. I had never been in a little rowboat on such a river, but the way Slim handled the oars and managed the craft eased most of my fears. When safe on the other side, I heaved a sigh of relief to have completed my long journey that began so many days ago.

As Slim secured the boat, I looked around and saw their homestead in the wildernes. The main cabin appeared cozy and homey, but it was built so close to the ground that it did not seem to have a regular foundation. The little cabin to the front side was perched on high stilts.

I asked why that one was so far off the ground while the other building was so low. They explained that the high one was a cache to keep out wolverines, which could not climb up stilts that were covered with tin. They had to tell me about wolverines and how they could wreck a cache. Then Slim explained that on the low building, the first log down was the foundation.

As we approached the yard, the dogs were barking and whining their joy at our arrival. Aileen introduced me to those wonderful Alaskan sled dogs, and I was enchanted. I adored them, and felt as if I were in heaven, with so many wagging tails. Then she took me over to see Hoppy, the wolf. His tail was not wagging as the dogs' were. He stood his distance as Aileen talked to him. He came over to her slowly and she petted his head, but he kept his eyes on me. We left him then, and went into the cabin. From Aileen's description of the cabin in her letters, I had the feeling that I had been there before, which gave me a sense of home. I loved it. It *was* my new home.

The following days were busy ones, getting me settled and familiar with the immediate area. I wanted to get to know Slim better, and so I began following him around, watching him at his tasks. One day we were down by the slough, which was about two feet deep, and I got a little feisty and sassed him for some direction he had given me. He just picked me up and calmly dropped me in the slough. I was astonished, and very wet. He then said to me, "I will have no kid sassing me. Now go and get dry." Of course I was quite angry and unhappy – dripping wet, cold, and biting back the tears. I went to my room and dried off, put on dry clothes, and went right back out to where Slim was working and said to him, "I'm sorry, I will never sass you again." He grinned at me and gave me a big hug. Then he explained that I must learn to respect any order given by either him or Aileen, for my own safety in this northern environment.

Slim was a very pleasant and cheerful man, always ready for a laugh. I only saw him angry once – no, twice – but the second was to come much later. The first time, someone called him on that big oak phone and told him that George Bellefontaine was down at Gakona and had said some bad things about Aileen. When he hung up the receiver, he grabbed his gun and, as he started for the boat, said, "I'll kill the son of a bitch." Aileen stood there stunned and called to him to stop. But he paid no attention to her, got in his boat, and rowed across the river. Aileen then called to Gakona and told them that Slim was on his way down there to kill George. The only thing we could do was just sit there and wait.

We were greatly relieved when Slim came back an hour later. He laughed at himself and said, "I got part of the way down and cooled off." Later that day, we heard two rifle shots across the river. It was George's signal for Slim to go over and get him. When they got to the house, George apologized to Aileen and handed her a fifty-dollar bill. She did not want to take it, but he kept insisting. Slim finally said, "Take the damn bill, Aileen, and finish this thing." She took it. After that episode, life with George popping in and out was more pleasant.

Soon after that, Slim began my lessons with the .22-caliber rifle. He showed me how to take it apart and

Samme and Beaver, carrying pack

clean it, and then how to shoot it. He nailed a tin can lid on a tree and showed me how to aim the gun and try to hit the target. I was to be confined to the home area until I was able to hit that lid at least eight times out of ten. When I accomplished that, after untold boxes of ammunition, he gave me Aileen's Savage 300 rifle and showed me how to use it. The first time I pulled the trigger, I fell over backward and landed on my behind. Slim stood there and had a good laugh and helped me to my feet. The next time I shot it, I braced myself and stood my ground. There was a lot of difference between the two guns. I liked the feel of the big rifle the best and spent much of my time practicing. It was a big thrill for me to be able to shoot a rifle and actually to become quite accurate. When Slim saw the progress I had made, he said, "Now you're ready to go."

Go, we did, the three of us with five excited pack dogs, four half-grown pups, and one too small to walk. Hoppy we left at home because we weren't sure what would happen if we turned him loose. Very little was known about wild wolves at the time, but we did know we couldn't put Hoppy on a leash. Neither Aileen nor I were strong enough to hold him. So we left him in the care of a neighbor.

This was my first adventure into the real wilderness, with a Savage 300 rifle on my back, a camera around my neck, and the puppy, Hudson, in my arms. We went up to Caribou Creek at the foot of Mount Sanford, to build a small cabin for the trapping season. The sled dogs carried our supplies in canvas packs that fit over their backs, with big pockets on each side. Slim tied the pack on the dog in such a way that the ropes would keep the pack balanced and steady but would not chafe the dog. The big dogs could carry about fifty pounds each, and were turned loose to follow us. As we trekked through the brush, Slim would find places to get through. If it was too thick, he would cut a path, or the dogs would get stuck with those packs sticking out on each side. Some of the trail was through open forest country without brush, which was much easier going.

I don't know how far it was to the building site, but it took us two long days of hiking to get there. The night we spent in the woods was some experience for me. Slim unpacked the dogs and tied them to trees as close to us as he could find. The pups would just stay with us and did not have to be tied up. Aileen and I gathered dry wood and made a campfire, so she could prepare our food – campfire bannock, beans, and bacon.

Slim and Aileen at Caribou Creek

After we had our supper, Slim made our bed by cutting down big spruce tree branches and piling them on top of each other. When he had a thick enough pile, he threw a canvas over them. Aileen said, "Well, come on, Samme. Let's fix our bed." She crawled onto the middle of the canvas fully dressed and stretched out on her back and began squirming around until she found a comfortable place. She indicated that I lie beside her. I did, and then I squirmed around until nothing poked me. Slim lay down on the other side of Aileen, and he didn't squirm, but pulled a big Hudson's Bay blanket over all of us and went right to sleep. It was my first night under the stars, and I lay awake much longer than my two spruce bough buddies.

After another day of hiking, Slim found the place to build the cabin. The creek widened out and there was room between the creek and the bank for our building. There was a meadow beyond the site, and Slim said, "This will give us easy access to the foot of the mountain, where we'll set the trap line." The mountain he referred to was the mighty Mount Sanford, one of the towering beauties of the Wrangell Mountains.

We lived in a tent while we built the little cabin, and cooked our food over a campfire like the real woodsmen we were. We had left Hoppy at home under George's care, but we had five dogs, four half-grown pups, and one small pup for entertainment.

During those days I began to learn how to use an axe. Slim would cut down a tree and Aileen and I would cut off the branches. A few of the trees grew at a slant up the bank, making it hard for Slim to fell them in the direction he wanted. So I would climb the tree and tie a rope around it, and Slim would secure the other end to another tree. That would give him the leverage he needed to bring the tree down where he wanted it. It may have been work for him, but it was a lot of fun for me. I might have been missing some reading, writing, and arithmetic, but I was certainly being educated on other subjects – how to build a log cabin, use an axe, climb a tree, build a fire in the rain, shoot a rifle, and live in the brush. I don't think they had any classes to teach those things at Fresno High.

We finished the cabin, and it was a small one. The roof was made waterproof with small poles, tarpaper, and moss. It measured about nine by twelve feet, just big enough for a bunk across the back and a Yukon stove and table in the front, which we brought up later on the sled. Slim built the bunk about three feet high and wide enough for the three of us. He covered it with small logs. "In the winter," he said, "we'll pile lots of blankets on those logs so it will be comfortable."

With that, our work was finished, and we packed up and left for home. On the way back it drizzled for two days. We were damp and cold most of the trip, but we stopped each day for tea. And it seemed that we could always find something to laugh about. On one of our last stops for rest and drink, I was letting my hot cup of tea cool down, holding it with both hands for warmth. I tilted my head down to get a sip, and the rainwater that had accumulated in my hat brim drained into my cup. That cooled it off enough for me to drink the tea, and I did, rainwater and all. When Aileen and Slim saw what had happened, they burst out laughing. Then we put out our campfire, called the dogs, and headed for home.

Hoppy was a very happy wolf when we arrived, and it felt good to reach our home at last. My first real wilderness adventure was over, and I was ready for a bath in a round washtub bought especially for such an occasion.

THE LONG JOURNEY

*D*uring the following days, we were busy getting ready for our next trip. Our leisure time was spent watching Hoppy. He loved to tease Goldie, a four-month-old pup. She evidently liked him, as she played a game with him over and over. She would gnaw on an old piece of caribou hide just close enough to Hoppy so he could snatch it away from her. When he did, she would attack him ferociously to retrieve her precious piece of hide. He would play tug-o-war with her, and when she was pulling the hardest, he would let go. This caused her to stumble backward, and when she got her balance, she would prance around with the trophy. She would then go right back to the same place, and the game would be replayed.

Goldie was one of four pups; the others were Monty, Bracken, and Bucky. They were such fun, and they followed us wherever we went. One day we took a hike along the Sanford River using the Frenchman's trail, and the four pups came along. We walked about a mile and turned back. When we got home, the pups followed us into the yard one by one. They had played and run back and forth on the trail, and they were tired. We soon realized that Bucky was missing. We didn't think much about it at first, but after an hour and no sign of Bucky, we were alarmed, so Slim went back up the trail calling him. After a long time, Slim returned alone. Slim thought perhaps an eagle had gotten the pup, or he had fallen down the cliff to the river. We, of course, were sad to lose him. Then, ten days later, to our great surprise Bucky staggered into the yard. He had no sign of abuse or injury on him, but when I tried to pick him up, he screamed. He was so tender I couldn't touch him. It was to remain a mystery that we would never solve. Those ten days he was gone, and whatever happened to him, had changed him. He had always been awkward and afraid, but now he was aggressive and able to hold his own. He turned out to be a strong sled dog.

There was always a lot to do and to see. We three enjoyed talking and working together. Sometimes Slim would take off through the back woods and be gone a couple of hours. One day I asked Aileen, "What does Slim do out there by himself for so long?" Aileen just smiled and said, "Oh, that's a secret."

Well, that really interested me. Who doesn't want to know a secret? "Will you tell me what it is?" I asked.

She gave me a Mona Lisa smile and replied, "Not now, but one day we will take you up and show you the se-

Samme's first caribou, Sanford River, 1927

cret." I would just have to wait until they were ready to reveal it to me.

Two weeks later Slim said, "Well, let's take a little hike out back." As we left the cabin, we went into thick brush with no sign of any trail. Slim was very careful not to break any foliage, and we sort of zigzagged our way. Suddenly we stopped in a small clearing, and there it was – a funny-looking bunch of coiled copper tubes, a big container placed over a campfire, and lots of bottles standing on a crude wooden table. I just looked and said, "Well, where's the secret?"

Slim said, "It's what is made here, that's the secret. This is a still and I make whiskey to sell. Right now it is part of our income."

Wow! I was surprised and said, "Is it against the law in Alaska?" He said that it was, and even though Alaska was a territory, prohibition was the law. That's why it was secret. Slim never went up to the still the same way twice. He did not drink it himself, but we had a little bottle at home and he would sometimes make a coffee royale for himself.

Now here's a funny thing in connection with this whiskey business. Whenever a revenue agent boarded the train in Cordova, the conductor would blow the whistle in a different way when the train arrived in Chitina. Then the word would go out with a coded message that the revenue agent was in the valley. He would travel up and down the Richardson Highway looking for moonshiners. Everyone along the trail kept an eye out for him and would report his whereabouts by phone. They had a code name for him, and his real name was never mentioned. Slim would never bring his whiskey down to the trail when the agent was abroad. He had a lot of customers, and they didn't want him to get caught. Slim made a good living that summer, from salmon and whiskey.

Remember the old saying about the cat and curiosity? Well, I should have remembered it when I found out about the whiskey. We had never had it at any time in our home in Fresno, and I became very curious about the taste of it. I asked Slim to let me sample it. He poured a little in a glass with some water, and handed it to me. Aileen practically screamed and tried to grab it out of my hand, but Slim intercepted. He said, " Let her try it here with us and she'll never be tempted to drink it again."

After drinking that one and then another, I was blotto. I went outside and the earth just came right up and got me. I struggled to my feet and staggered out to my favorite dog, Sonki. I put my arms around him, hugged and kissed him, and then got very sick. Aileen took care of me, but she didn't speak to Slim for the rest of the day. You know, it did teach me this: I never took another drink of whiskey again.

One day in late August, Slim rushed into the cabin and said, "Samme, get your outdoor clothes on as fast as possible. I just saw a small herd of caribou down on the mouth of the Sanford River. Now is your time to shoot a caribou."

I got my clothes changed, and Slim handed my gun to me as I went out the door. We walked down the Copper and around the bluff, and there was the herd. Very quietly we approached them, and when we were within firing range, Slim whispered as he pointed, "Now just be very quiet and take very careful aim at the shoulder of that caribou."

It was a big animal closest to us. I knelt down, took careful aim, and fired. My quarry did not flinch, but her calf a bit in front of her fell dead. I felt horrified to have killed a calf, and Slim stood there trying to keep from laughing out loud. While he was doing that, I aimed again and downed the big animal. It was my first hunting experience, and I felt a little sense of pride. Slim was proud of me too, for after all, I was his pupil.

We took pictures of me with my first caribou, and you could see how delighted I was with my accomplishment. After Slim showed me how to gut the animal and clean it out, we got the dogs and sled to bring the meat into the yard.

Slim and Aileen had trapped the previous season over on the Gakona River, leaving some useful gear there. Preparation for the trip to retrieve it took a lot of time, because we would be gone about a month. We planned to leave on the first of September when summer heat was over and the mosquitoes were gone. It was a good time of the year to travel in the woods. The beauty of the fall colors was beginning to appear more each day, but the days and nights still had some of the summer warmth left.

Slim had a friend, Mike Cotter, who came to look after Hoppy and stay at the cabin. He also helped us get across the Copper, which was the first leg of our journey. It took three trips in the rowboat to get seven pack dogs, five pups, and three humans over to the other side of the river. We went single file up to the road, turned right, and finally were on our way.

The road had been cleared and graded, although it was just dirt ruts. It was easy going for about eight miles until it ended. Then we had to make our way through the brush using the old Eagle Trail, as far as Chistochina. That first night we found an old cabin for shelter. It was quite a chore to make camp. All the dogs had to be unpacked, tied up, and fed. Wood had to be gathered for the campfire, and beds had to be prepared. By the time all that was done, we were ready to "hit the hay," only in this case there was no hay.

The next day we reached Chistochina Roadhouse, where we had our dinner with Red Hurst, the proprietor. It would be the last meal we would have indoors for a long time. We slept upstairs on a regular bed, under a regular roof, and that was the last time we did so for many nights.

Samme and Slim crossing a glacial stream,
Chistochina, Alaska, 1927

The long journey began the following day. We headed up along the Chistochina River into the wilderness where no trails existed. There were dead logs to step over, brush to push aside, river rocks to walk on, moss to sink into, and streams to ford. Many times the dogs had to be helped over big logs or through tangled brush. It was extremely rough. A number of times we crossed the river as it twisted its way down to the Copper. We didn't stop to dry out but just kept going. I carried the smallest pup, Hudson, because he was too little to walk through that brush or wade the streams. Finally we put him in Sonki's pack, and his little head bounced up and down with the gait of the big dog. We were exhausted at the end of each day.

After four days heading up the Chistochina, we turned our direction to the west and headed for the Gakona River.

If the previous days were rough, this part of the trip was hellish. For miles we had to struggle through deep moss, which was like walking on soft, deep sand. I almost caved in on that march, which was the most difficult part of the entire trip. I had to clench my jaws down hard to keep from crying. When we got to the Gakona River, we were very close to the old campsite. It was a wonderful feeling to have our destination in view, after the difficult journey we had made. In the camp at last, we slumped down and rested. Slim announced, "No more of that moss – we'll go back a different way."

During this trip, I realized an interesting thing about the dogs – they reflected our moods. If we were tired, they were tired. If we felt peppy and light-hearted, so did they. Most of the time they were obedient and ready to please.

The gear that we picked up at the old camp included a tent and a Yukon stove. They would make our return trip a little more comfortable. It was getting colder every day, and shore ice was beginning to form on the little streams. The shelter of the tent and warmth of the Yukon stove would be welcome.

The morning we left for our return journey, it was sunny and warm. We headed up the Gakona River to find a higher pass on which to cross back over to the Chistochina. At this point, the river was spread out in little streams about a mile across. Moss covered the bank, along with a few clumps of scrub brush.

By now our supply of dog food was getting short and Slim reminded us to look for game. It was about ten o'clock when Aileen, with her long-distance vision, spotted a caribou on the other side of the river. He had evidently seen us, as he was walking toward us at about the two o'clock position. It was mating season, and the male caribou will slowly walk toward anything that moves. We prepared for him as he advanced. Slim gathered the big dogs around him, and I took charge of the pups to keep them quiet. Aileen got herself in a position to shoot. She was about a foot forward and three feet to the left of me. We all had our eyes on the approaching caribou that was still out of shooting range. The sun was at about ten o'clock, and no one was looking in that direction. I happened to glance at Aileen, and just beyond her on the other side of a small channel of the river, with his back to the sun, stood another big male caribou. He was well within shooting range. I whispered to Aileen, "Why don't you get that one?" She slowly turned, and downed him with one shot.

Slim butchered the caribou, got what he wanted for us, and let the dogs loose to feed on the meat. What a show it was! Each dog approached the food in a different way. Bucky was determined to have it all and was more concerned with keeping it than eating it. Klute sat back and watched the others grabbing and growling, then she darted in, got a piece, and went away by herself. Beaver and Sonki almost came to blows over one special piece, but they were too hungry to fight. None of those dogs had ever had the opportunity to feast on a carcass before. Watching them was better than an entire circus.

After all the dogs were fed, we took what meat we could carry and moved on up the river. Eventually Slim found a flat, mossy place to pitch the tent for the night. The Yukon stove provided us with warmth and fresh caribou stew. We got very little sleep that night. Slim was stationed by the stove to keep the fire going, and I stayed outside where

Crossing Slate Creek Pass, fall 1927

it was cold. Slim got too hot by the stove, and I got too cold away from the heat, so we would switch places, passing over Aileen in the middle. She couldn't sleep, either, for bodies crossing over her all night long.

It snowed that night and in the morning, and the world looked different with its new dress of white. It was my first snow, and I was thrilled to see it and touch it. More ice was forming on the edges of the streams; these signs of approaching winter were new to me, and the beauty of the changing landscape was captivating.

That morning we walked a few miles farther up the Gakona and then turned toward the Chistochina River, crossing over the Slate Creek Pass. It was high country, and there was no moss or brush. The trail was good, and where it began to follow the slope down to the river, we found an old deserted cabin that had belonged to someone named Dempsey. A rusty beat-up stove was the only thing in it, but it was shelter and warmth and we were grateful for that. We stayed there a couple of nights to dry out and rest for the journey ahead of us.

Our return down to the Chistochina Roadhouse took many days. It was just as hard coming down the river as it was going up. By now, it was colder and the sun was going down a little earlier. We were getting closer to home with each step, and the desire to be back in the comfort and security of our own little cabin kept us going.

As we neared the roadhouse, I ran ahead to see if there was smoke coming out of the chimney. At a turn in the path, I could see the building and the welcome sight of smoke above it, which meant that Red Hurst was home! I had been in the woods for almost a month, and that was enough. For dinner that night, we had freshly cooked bacon and beans, biscuits, and canned peaches. I hadn't had anything sweet since we had left home, so I put strawberry preserves on my beans. It was like a feast to me, and it tasted heavenly.

The next day we left for the final leg of our long journey. We arrived at our path to the river two days later, after dark. Slim had some lanterns cached there for just such an occasion. These lanterns were unique; he had made them out of one-pound lard buckets. A hole for the candle was cut in the side of the bucket. A handle was fixed over the other side of the bucket, and when it was carried, the light shone ahead out of the top. We lit our candles and went slowly down the hill to the boat. Slim and Aileen unpacked the dogs, fed them each a dried salmon, and tied them on that side of the river, where we would return to retrieve them the next day. We did take the pups, but it was dark and we were too tired to face the ordeal of getting us all across the river that night. That final crossing of the river in the inky blackness was the most terrifying event of the entire trip. When we reached the shore, I was the first out of the boat and gave out a whoop of relief.

Hoppy was excited to see us, and the pups ran to him. With the light from our lanterns, we could see Hoppy and the pups greeting each other with much licking and wagging. As tired as she was, Aileen went to the wolf to pet him. That night, after we had gone to bed, we heard a strange noise at the door. Slim investigated, and there was Sonki, dripping wet. He had gotten loose and had swum the river to get home. Slim dried him off as well as he could and let him sleep inside that night, because outside it was too cold for a wet dog.

As I was going to sleep, I remembered the little prayer, "Now I lay me down to sleep," and I was grateful to be safe in my own bed again. That long journey ended my second adventure in the wilderness of Alaska.

FOURTEEN HOURS

*A*s the days became shorter, storms raged, and snow got deeper, we spent most of our time in the cabin. We enjoyed those leisure times. There was always something to do. Aileen might read a good story to us, or while we were baking or cooking, we would play word games such as "Initials." Slim loved to tell us of his hair-raising experiences. Painting with pastels kept me busy, and occasionally I studied some schoolbooks I had brought. We talked about trips we could take, such as going to Dawson in the Yukon Territory.

Later, the storms began to be less frequent, and many of the winter days were sunny. The sun on the snow turned our world into a fairyland of sparkling wonder.

Samme with dog team

It was enchanting, and I wanted to make snowballs, but snow in Interior Alaska is so dry that I couldn't make even a little one.

"During this break in the weather, I want to go up the bank of the river to look for fur sign," Slim announced. He turned to me and said, "Samme, would you like to come with me? You could drive the dogs while I go ahead on snowshoes to make the trail."

Of course I said, "Yes." Manning the sled would be good training for me. I would have no trouble driving

the dogs, as they would just follow Slim.

The morning we left, the sky was clear with no sign of bad weather. We left about nine o'clock, and Slim told Aileen we would be gone about five hours. Off we went up the bank and through the woods.

It was easy going until we came to muskeg swamps. Covered with snow, the tussocks appeared smooth, but they were rough to get across. Between their solid stalks, the snow was soft and the dogs had a hard time getting their footing. The snowshoe trail that Slim was making didn't help, so the dogs and I had to struggle to get the sled through. The swamps were only about a hundred yards across but there were many of them, so by noon the dogs and I needed a rest. I yelled for Slim to stop, and he came back. He said, "We've only come about six miles, and I'd like to go a few miles farther." So we rested a few minutes and kept going.

A rise in the land made the going easier, as there were no more swamps. We had gone for about another hour when Slim came back to the sled and said, "I think we've come far enough. I'll look for a place where we can get down to the river, then we'll head for home on the ice and be there in no time."

It took him a long time, though, before he could find a way down to the river. When he did, I was relieved that he took over the job of getting the dogs and sled down through the thick brush. I stumbled along behind. It was good to be on the river with an easy trail. He told me to get in the sled, and off we went.

I was relaxing from my hard day's trek when all of a sudden Slim slammed on the brakes. The sled skidded around and ice spewed. He yelled for me to get out of the sled and hold the brakes as he ran to the front to help Stub, who was in the river's open channel. He got her out and wiped off the icy water as best he could. The open channel had cut across the river and slashed into the bank. It was about twelve feet of open, rushing water, hard to see until you were right on it.

Slim got the dogs turned around and said, "We'll have to go back up the bank. There's no way across the channel." We took to the bank again and struggled through the thick vegetation, with Slim going ahead to move the brush so I could get the sled through. After what seemed like a long time, he said that he could see the river, and that it was clear for travel. It was quite dark, and the only light we had was a quarter moon, but it reflected on the snow and gave us fair visibility, at least enough to struggle down through the brush once again to the river.

Due to an overflow, there was about an inch of water on the ice. We could travel on that without any danger, but I had a different problem – I had to relieve my bladder. I told Slim that I couldn't wait, so he fixed me a place. We both stood on his snowshoes, which kept me out of the water. I was wearing coveralls that unfastened from the top. First, I had to take off my jacket; next, unbutton my coverall straps and hand them to Slim; then, pull my pants down and bare my behind. Slim held my clothes while I squatted at his feet. This was a shattering embarrassment for me, a fifteen-year-old girl. Of course, being the man that he was, he never gave up teasing me about the episode. He claimed that I had baptized his snowshoes.

The river was not kind to us that day. We had gone a short distance when the channel again broke out in front of us. This time we could see it as it came across at an angle and tore into the bank, forcing us to take to the brush again. Slim cached the sled, unloosed the dogs, and went ahead. I followed, and the dogs came behind. They walked as close to me as they could, as though they wanted to lean against me.

I don't remember how long we fought our way through that miserable situation, but we did somehow get back down to the river. We were still about two miles from home. At that point, I was exhausted and began to whimper. When I did, Slim began to call me names – a quitter, a baby, stupid, and such. I really don't remember all he said, but it shocked and angered me. I stopped whimpering and plodded on, one step at a time.

Finally we staggered into the cabin. It was eleven o'clock, and Aileen was frantic by this time. She had called below to report the situation, and they were on standby. We had been gone fourteen hours. It had been an ordeal I would never want to repeat; I was numb, and Aileen had to undress me, as my hands would not work and my eyes were set in a stare. The experience taught me that in this country, when you leave home in the morning you cannot always foresee what will happen to you before nightfall.

Slim apologized the next day for calling me those names. He said, "If I had sympathized with you, you'd have folded up. I would have had to carry you, and I was too exhausted to do that." He added, "I'd say you were one great gal." I smiled.

CHANNEL ICE

*D*uring the fall, storms brought deep snow and river ice began to form. While we could still get over the river in the boat, we made a few trips to Gakona, taking the road by foot. But as the river ice got thicker, it became unsafe for crossing. The channel is the portion of the river where the water never stops flowing. On each side of the channel the river may be frozen solid, but until a sheet of ice forms over the top of the channel there is no way to cross. We waited patiently for nature to take its own time, and after a few weeks or so, Slim reported that the channel was frozen over.

Now we could go down to Gakona for the mail. We got ourselves ready, hitched the dogs to the sled, and joyfully took off for a trip to the post office, crossing the channel on solid ice and heading up the road. This time of year, we would stay overnight at the roadhouse. It was a change, and we always enjoyed any company that we would find there.

That night a Chinook, a warm wind, caused a thaw that changed the ice condition on the river. When we arrived at our previous crossing on the way home the next day, the channel ice looked different. Instead of being smooth and solid as it was yesterday, it was rough and crinkled. Slim examined and tested it. He said, "If we go straight across, it will be safe."

I got on the nose of the sled with Aileen behind me, and Slim was on the back runners. He called, "Mush," and Stub began to lead the team straight across. We crossed the channel, but as the first quarter of the sled nosed back onto solid ice, Stub turned up a ridge, which we hadn't seen from the other side. This turn of the sled caused the runner to jab into the ridge, and the ice under the rest of the sled all gave way.

Aileen screamed, and for a moment I was too shocked to move. Slim yelled as he dropped into icy water up to his chest. He held the sled up as best he could for us to get off, but he had no footing. I went first and grabbed the bow as I stepped over it. Aileen got off onto some ice that still held, then crawled onto something more solid. The dogs were holding against the backward pull of the sled. We could hear their nails digging into the ice. Aileen yelled at Stub to pull, and together with the dogs, we were able to get the sled out of the water and onto solid ice. Slim, almost too cold to function, pulled himself out of that icy grave with the help of the sled. He was drenched from his

In front of the roadhouse at Gakona, Alaska. Al Norwood, Herb Hyland, Tommy Hyke, Eugenia Brown, Arne Sundt

neck to his feet. We were close to the cabin, so we made a dash for home.

No one said much about the experience, as we were still in a state of shock. We could all easily have perished in that icy river. When Slim was all dried off and in warm clothes, he came in and sat by the stove. Reaching up to his left shirt pocket where he always kept his tobacco, he took a deep breath and said, "Damn, I got my Bull Durham wet."

CARIBOU CREEK

*I*n the winter of 1928, we trapped on the slope of Mount Sanford, and lived in the little cabin we had built the previous fall on Caribou Creek. The trip up to the cabin took us many long hours. The sled was heavily loaded with supplies and Klute's five puppies. This meant that we all walked. It was dark when we got to the cabin, and all of us, even the pups, were dead-tired. After eating some bread and jam with tea, we went to bed.

The word "bed" generally denotes comfort, but this bed spelled sore shoulders, head, back, and sore everything. The bunk was made of small logs laid close to each other, horizontally to the sleeper. Boughs of spruce branches were placed over the logs, and on top of that a heavy canvas. A couple of quilts under us helped to ease the discomfort a little.

We had to let the pups sleep inside that first night, and they cried for their mother nearly the whole night. Weary the next day, the first thing we did was to build a bed for Klute and those pups right outside the door. They were special to me, as I was there when they were born. One of them was so beautiful, I said, "He looks like a Rembrandt painting." So we named him Rembrandt, but called him Brandt.

The cabin was very small for three people, especially when one was a man as big as Slim. It was nine by twelve feet, and the bunk took up almost half the floor space. A little Yukon stove was in one corner, and a rickety table filled the other. For chairs, we sat on the bunk. When we arrived, the dirt floor was frozen like everything else. But when our fire started to warm up, the floor began to thaw out. So what did we have then? Why, mud, of course. A *Good Housekeeping Magazine* editor would have fainted dead away at the mess.

The one window was very small but gave us a little light. The door opening was almost square, being only slightly higher than it was wide, and we had to step up about a foot to get in or out. Slim had to both step up and bend down, because of his height. He had built the cabin, though, so he didn't complain. Our door covering, a piece of heavy canvas with a heavy blanket hung over it at night, was adequate to keep out the cold. To a fifteen-year-old city girl, it was a glorious camping trip. I loved the whole atmosphere of Caribou Creek, Mount Sanford, the intense cold, the log cabin, the snow, the dogs, the wolf, and most of all, the puppies.

Caribou Creek cabin

Aileen and I got things in order in the camp area when Slim went out to set his traps. Once that was done, he checked the traps every day, weather permitting, and I got to go with him most of the time. If I didn't go, Aileen would go with him, and sometimes we would all go.

It was a big help for Slim to have one of us control the dogs while he took care of the traps. The team was usually very manageable, but there was always a chance that the dogs might see some caribou and give chase. With our help, Slim could get over the trap line in considerably less time than it would have taken him alone.

We had to work as fast as possible, for there were only a few hours of daylight. When there is no moon in Alaska, the nights are profoundly black, so we had to hurry to get home before dark. When there was moonlight, however, it shone brightly on the snow and made it easier to navigate.

On those long nights, we were happy to be in the cabin. Our wonderful Coleman lamp gave us light enough for Aileen to read us a story from the *Saturday Evening Post* before bed. Then we were up before daylight and ready to go at first light.

One morning I got to drive the dogs alone on a trail that wound up the mountain beside Caribou Creek. Slim had gone on ahead, and I had followed. When I caught up, about a mile later, he took over the sled.

That day as we were leaving for the cabin, we heard wolves howling. When we got to the top of a ridge, we saw two of them about a half-mile away. It was chilling to see wolves that close, but there were only two of them and we had two guns. Just before we went down the hill to the creek, we stopped and saw the wolves pass over the hill.

Slim said, "They're going down to my traps, and if there's a fox in one, they will probably destroy it." We watched them go down the ridge and across the hill heading straight to the traps, which were still some distance away. When they went out of sight, I was relieved, but suddenly they came running back up the hill, and I just froze. Now there were seven of them, but we still just had our two guns.

They were about a mile from us, so we descended into the gully and cut across the ridge. Dropping down again to the creek, we managed to get to the traps before the wolves. There were red foxes in two of them. Slim told me to hold the dogs while he got them out of the trap and put them on the sled. Back up on to the ridge, the wolves were still over on the hill watching us. When we turned to go home, they ran down the hill and up to the opposite ridge, trotting to keep pace with us. They were less than a mile away, across the small gully. I sat on the side of the sled and kept my eyes intently on them. Occasionally the pack would stop and have a howling session. Then they would run to keep across from us. They were there until we left the mountain and dropped down into the creek, where we headed for the cabin.

Even though Slim had assured me that we were in no danger from the wolves, I was very glad to be home in the little cabin in the woods. During that night the wolves howled from time to time, and when they did, our wolf, Hoppy, would join them. Soon all the dogs would begin their song. The ruckus would die down for a while and then start up again. It reminded me that they were still out there, and I would sink lower into the covers. The next day they were gone, and we never saw them again.

Several days later, Slim had to go down to the home cabin for supplies. He came back with a wonderful treat – a mattress! We put it on the bunk and finally had solid comfort. I do mean solid, but it was better than the spruce boughs. It is a fact that when you are very tired, sleep comes fast and bodily discomfort does not interfere – well, not much.

At the bottom of Mount Sanford glacier, we killed two caribou. It took some time to clean them and bring them to the camp where we hung them on a tree to freeze solid. We had caribou stew for supper, and it was a relief to have something to eat besides bacon and beans. The dogs had a feast, for they too needed a change of diet.

That morning we heard a fox barking close to camp. The dogs became excited, and Hoppy ran around in a frenzy. Slim checked it out and found fox tracks within one hundred feet of our area. He thought the fox had smelled fresh meat and had hoped to get some. Later we returned to where we had killed the caribou and there was hardly any trace of leavings. The wolf pack had evidently eaten every scrap we left there.

One morning Aileen and I walked up on the slope of Mount Sanford. It was a bright winter day with our whole world in view. We could see the great Copper River Valley spread out below us. Across to the north we could see the majestic Alaska Range. We stood in awe of the glorious sight. Aileen said, "You know, I think we are the only people who have ever been right here before."

I replied, "And the only people with such dirty necks." With that, we began laughing at ourselves, two California city girls standing at the bottom of a glacier with Mount Sanford rising majestically above us. We had guns on our backs, moccasins on our feet, shells in our pockets, and grins on our faces. This was the best day of my life in Alaska. It tied Aileen and me together with a very strong love for each other, and I have never forgotten it.

When the season ended, we packed up to go back to our Copper River homesite. The sled was loaded with pelts, so we all had to walk. This time the pups were big enough to follow along, and if one of them seemed tired, someone would carry it. Our cabin was a very welcome sight.

We were happy to be back with our comforts, and who wouldn't be glad, if one hadn't changed clothes, hadn't washed anything but hands and face, or hadn't slept on a soft bed for three weeks. It took us a few days to get everything clean and back to normal. Slim took the skins down to the fur buyer at Gakona. It had been a good season, and now we could relax until the salmon run in June.

It was still dogsled time and we made the most of it, making many fun trips to visit the folks at Gakona, Gulkana, and Copper Center, and going up to Sourdough to visit old Doc Blaylock.

The pups were bright and lively. They were six months old when Klute began to wean them. Now they had to be fed, and Slim called them the "Little Suckers." They were the center of my life, and I helped with their early training. Brandt was still the most beautiful dog I had ever seen, and he was a fast learner. His brother was named Patagonia, but we called him Pat. He was gray and a little shaggy, and smart like Brandt. I loved to go out to the dogs every day. They were eager to have me sit down with them. They loved the hugs and affection that I gave them. Slim said I had the choice of either petting them or driving them. I said that I'd rather pet them, but, you know, I was able to do both.

One evening I saw the faint pink glow of northern lights. They danced and shot out and up, dimmed and grew brighter. They were fascinating, and it became my pastime to watch every night for them. Another novel sight I saw was Red Hurst driving his Ford along on the river ice. There were few roads in the Copper River Valley in the late twenties. The highway from Valdez to Fairbanks had been built, and also a road to Chitina. A road from Gakona to Chistochina was under construction, going only twenty miles before stopping abruptly in the middle of the forest. The only way Red could drive his Ford from Chistochina down to Gakona was on the river ice.

One day he stopped and had lunch with us and then drove off again. Later that evening he came back again with Susie and Ralph, two Natives. They had coffee and cake with us, and we all went out and looked at the Ford. When they finally left, Hoppy just ran around and around his circle as fast as he could go. I think the sound of the engine alarmed him.

There were others who came by that winter. Arne Sundt arrived one day with his wagon and horses to ask Slim if I could ride up the river with him, if I wanted to go. Slim said that I could. It was one more adventure, so off I went on the big wagon with the big Norwegian. When you're sixteen, anyone older than twenty seems old, and I thought of him as an old man, but when he giggled and laughed and acted like a schoolboy, I realized he was not all that old. He helped me up on the sled and we sat side by side. He didn't touch me or say anything romantic, but later Arne asked Slim if he could marry me. Slim said, "No."

Nobody asked *me.*

SPRINGTIME

*I*t is a big day in Alaska when the rivers let go their winter cloaks of ice and springtime comes again. As the days got warmer, the ice, of course, started thawing. Travel on the river diminished as the channel got larger and the ice got softer. To see the Copper lose its burden of ice would be a onetime event for me, as I would be going home in July and we figured perhaps I would never see it happen again. Daily I watched the changes. Some days there would be little activity, then the next day there would be grinding and popping sounds, and water would flow out of cracks in the ice. Then one afternoon in early May that mass of ice suddenly began to move. It churned and cracked, and great chunks reared up and then banged down.

Aileen and Copper River salmon

What a sight! And what a noise! It was one of the most thrilling things I had ever seen.

Then, after a few days, when the river was clear of ice, it flowed along in its channel just as though nothing had ever happened. It's difficult to describe, like the northern lights – you have to see it to believe it.

After the river was flowing normally and the salmon began to head upstream to their spawning grounds, it was time to install the fish wheel. Slim set it up on a tripod in the Copper River about two feet from the bank. As the current turned it, the big wheel, which had two large buckets attached, scooped up fish and tossed them into a floating box right beside the contraption. At the peak of the season, each turn of the wheel yielded about two fish per revolution and we rejoiced.

Slim had made drying racks, and we got busy cleaning the fish for curing. We were catching about a thousand pounds a day, and we worked day and night to keep up with the flow. However, it did not seem like work to us. We sang and talked and just had fun. And did we eat salmon? I'll say we did. We feasted on salmon, new potatoes that we had grown, and butter. We also had fresh lettuce and rhubarb from our garden.

After the fish were dried, we stored them in the high cache — a storage room built on stilts to keep animals from robbing it — to use for feeding the dogs. Besides being delicious food for both humans and our team, salmon was a source of income for Slim and Aileen, as there was a good market for it in the winter.

One day after Slim took inventory of the dried fish, he announced that there had been a thief in the night. Something was stealing our salmon. He thought it was a bear, and he said he'd have to get it. There was a little log cabin alongside the salmon drying racks, and he decided to spend the night there and wait for the thief. I asked him if I could stay and get the bear, and he agreed to let me do it, *alone*!

There was a little opening about four inches square on one side of the cabin. Slim fixed a place where I could sit with the gun partly out the hole. There was light almost all night, so if the bear came in sight, I could shoot it. With a blanket for warmth, a box for a back support, and a stopwatch (for what, I don't remember), I was ready for my vigil.

I waited, I measured the long seconds with my stopwatch, and I waited some more. As the night dragged on, the only thing that I saw in the sights of my gun was a skinny coyote. He stopped and looked around, then sauntered on out of sight and was gone for a long time. Then he came back and his sides were bulging out. I didn't shoot him, because I was waiting for a bear. Well, one never came, and did Slim and Aileen ever laugh when they heard about the coyote, and so did I. Too late, I had realized the identity of the robber. One thing I learned in that cabin, besides the length of a second on a stopwatch, was to expect the unexpected.

After the fishing season was over, we decided to do some visiting. Slim was acquainted with Dan Whitehead, who managed the roadhouse in Paxson, and we drove over there to see him. To my joy and surprise, his daughter and grandchildren were there. It was the first time in almost a year that I had seen people my own age. Danne, Grace, and John Meggitt were in their teens, and we had a great time together. John was the first boy I had talked to in a year, and of course I fell in love with him. He also felt the same way about me, and we began a correspondence that lasted for a year.

While we were visiting, Dan heard that I made a great sweet potato pie, and asked me if I would bake six of them for him. The tourist bus stopped once or twice a week for lunch at the Paxson Roadhouse, and my pies would be dessert. It was a big order for me, but I did make the pies. I almost burned them, but they turned out very well. Before leaving that day, we discovered that we teenagers were all booked to sail on the same ship the next July. The Meggitts would be traveling as far as Juneau, where they lived, and I would go on to Seattle, then California.

Later, after we had returned to the Copper River cabin, John walked up the seven miles from Gakona to see us.

We all talked late into the night, and John told us of his ambitions and dreams. It was a night of magic to me, even though we were not alone. Toward morning, Slim rowed John back across the river, and I didn't see him again until July.

Toward the end of my stay, Aileen and Slim came out into the yard where I was playing with the pups, and Aileen asked me if I would like to take one home. I was so overcome that I started to cry. "Oh yes, I would," I said. She knew that I was already having trouble about leaving the dogs, so they had decided that I could have one. I could choose one of Klute's wonderful pups. That was not easy, as I loved them all, but I chose a male and named him Paxson, after the roadhouse and because I had met John Meggett there.

We made one more trip into the woods before it was time for my return to Fresno. Slim had an old friend, Lawrence De Witt, and his wife, Belle, who lived up the Copper River at Slana. Slim said that he would like to see him, so we left one morning. It was sixty miles up there, but what the heck, we could do that in three days using the old Eagle trail.

It turned out that the trail was not so easy going. In many places the brush had obliterated the path, and moss covered it. Our strongest pack dog, Beaver, came with us. We stayed the first night in the same little dirty cabin we had used before. When we crossed the Chistochina River close to where it flows into the Copper, Slim carried the pack over and then came back for Aileen and me. Beaver swam across and was waiting for us on the bank. We locked hands with Slim by holding each other's wrists. He was in the middle, and the three of

John Meggett with his sisters, Grace and Danne

us waded across the river. I gasped as the cold water hit my groin and then my waist. Aileen was also making "cold water" sounds. It was a very dangerous situation, as the footing was rocky and the water was swift. It's a wonder we made it, but we did, and then we just kept walking. One more night in the open, and we reached Slana the third day, in the late afternoon. We stayed two nights.

Aileen and I enjoyed Belle and her baby boy, Angus. He had been born in October of 1927 and, since I loved little babies, I spent most of my time bouncing Angus.

In the meantime, Lawrence and Slim had found an old government boat in the bushes by the river. It was in bad shape, as the boards had come apart in many places. They fixed it by lashing a canvas under the whole structure of the boat and tying it securely in place. That was our transportation home, a canvas-bottom boat. The four of us (including the dog) got into that boat and floated down the Copper River. It was an unusual experience, and I wrote a poem about it.

THE CANVAS-BOTTOM BOAT

In a little canvas-bottom boat it was so hard to keep afloat.
Floating down the river, our hearts were all a-quiver
In a little canvas-bottom boat.

There were just three of us, four with Beaver, the old cuss.
He wouldn't keep still, and he nearly caused a spill
In a little canvas-bottom boat.

Once we got stuck on a bar, it wasn't for very far.
Oh, God he give us the right to live,
In a little canvas-bottom boat.

Finally we did get ashore, I'll tell you I don't want anymore.
I'd rather be a squatter than to live on the water,
In a little canvas-bottom boat.

There were channels so shallow our boat would almost become stuck. When the land crowded the river into a narrow channel, we would find ourselves in rapids. The seagulls nesting along the shallow channels were annoyed at our presence. The mother birds would pretend they were crippled, dragging their wings along and limping to draw attention away from their extremely ugly babies. Many places on the river were just lovely as we glided along with ease. And we arrived home in less time than it had taken us to go.

Then, too soon it was time for me to pack up my things and go home to California. Slim said, "I'm going to take Samme's trunk down to the landing at Gakona in the boat, so I won't have to carry it up to the car." When it was packed, Slim and I took it downriver in the canvas-bottom boat, and Aileen drove the car down to pick us up.

We arrived at the landing near Gakona, and after Slim had put the trunk on the bank, he started to shove the boat into the river. I asked him why he would do that. He said that it was still government property, and he didn't want to be caught with it. I took courage and said, "Push it up into the willows, because you never know when it might be needed." Imagine me telling him what to do, but he agreed and hid it against the bank. Aileen arrived with the car, and we drove over to Gulkana.

About one hour later, an airplane crashed on the Copper River near Gakona. It had landed on an island covered with driftwood that cushioned the impact. No one was killed, but the pilot and two passengers were badly injured. The river there was very swift as it flowed around the island. Two men tried to cross the channel in a rescue attempt, but they were half drunk and swamped their boat, almost drowning. The call went out for Slim, as he

Valdez, Alaska, from the dock, 1928

was known to be a good river man. As soon as he was located at Gulkana, he rushed to the site of the crash, which was directly across from where the little canvas-bottom boat was hidden in the willows. Slim pulled it out and with that little boat was able to rescue the three people who were injured. My hunch to save it had been a good one. After the rescue, Slim hid it again, and it may still be there.

The next few days went by much faster than the night I had waited for the bear. All the plans for my homeward trip were in order. My parents and my sister Una would meet me when my ship docked in Seattle. It was hard to say goodbye to Hoppy, to the dogs and pups, to my Copper River home, and most of all to Slim and Aileen. However, it had to be, as I needed to get on with my education. But I had my puppy, Paxson, and I also longed to see Mother.

In July we drove to Copper Center where we met Danne, Grace, and John. We all squeezed into the car and drove to Valdez, where we would board the ship. It was a bittersweet time for me – bitter because of leaving Aileen and Slim, and sweet because I would have a few hours with John. Aileen and Slim saw that Paxson and I were settled on the ship, then, as they went down the gangplank to the dock, tears streamed down my cheeks. The *SS Aleutian* left the harbor, and Aileen and Slim stood on the dock, waving and watching until we were out of sight. As I watched them fading in the distance, I thought something would break inside of me.

MY DOG, PAXSON

*W*hen I arrived in Seattle, my folks were there
to meet me. They almost collapsed when I
got Paxson from the freight department of
the ship. My father said, "How in the hell are we going
to drive with that huge animal?" He was a big puppy,
almost sixty pounds.

Well, when I started to cry, Mother said, "For God's
sake, Roy, she's been gone a year, we can certainly man-
age somehow."

So the five of us, which included Paxson, piled into
the touring car and headed for California. Paxson took
up as much room as any one of us. In those days the cars
had no glass windows. They were all open, and Paxson
kept trying to jump out. The trip home took us longer than

Samme and Paxson

expected, because we needed to make long stops for the dog. I began to learn that life in Alaska with big sled dogs was different than driving with one in the States.

When we finally reached home, Paxson was the talk of the town. The reporters from the *Fresno Bee* took our picture, and we were famous for a few weeks. The neighborhood folks all came to see the Alaskan sled dog, and he loved it. Everyone could pet him and shake hands with him.

My father made a good house for him in the backyard and chained him there. We couldn't let him run loose. He came inside when I was there, and knocked things down. His breed was not accustomed to little tables, chairs, and lamps, so he was outside most of the time. This was the pattern of our life until the fall, and he was a few months older. One morning when I went outside to see Paxson, I was astonished to see five dead chickens in the yard near his kennel. He was sitting there with a sense of pride, as though he had done something great. I called my father, and, oh boy, was he mad.

He quickly buried all the chickens, and was just finishing up when a furious neighbor stormed into the yard. He was ready to murder that "damned dog." My father calmed him down and said he would pay for the chickens.

From then on, it went from bad to worse. Whenever Paxson got loose, there were dead chickens in the yard. He never ate them. He just killed them. I don't know how much my father paid out for dead chickens. One woman even put up a seven-foot fence and reported that she saw Paxson just sail right over it — "like a deer."

One day I came home from school and went to the back to pet Paxson, as was my habit, and the kennel and my dog were not there. I ran in the house crying for Mother. She held me in her arms and told me that my father had found a good place for him out on a ranch close to the hills. It was a good place for the dog, as he could run free. I knew this was the only solution to the present problem with Paxson, but a little part of my heart broke off. I never saw him again. I could not go out to the ranch, pet and love him, and then walk away from him — so I just locked up my feelings and didn't look back.

PART III

Aileen Gallaher

1928

THE THIRD YEAR

*T*he trip home from Valdez was not a happy one for either Slim or me. We both missed Samme and her chatter. I hadn't realized what a difference it would make not to have her with us. We had depended on her presence to keep things lively. We were both very quiet, as though we didn't know what to say, and just drove along in silence.

When we reached home, the dogs jumped around for attention, and we greeted them. Then something happened that made me sad again. They kept looking back toward the boat as though they expected Samme. They watched for her for some time, but finally gave up and went back to sleep. Hoppy watched long after the dogs did.

Well, she was gone, I told myself, and there was nothing we could do about it. So I called Slim and said, "Get yourself in here. Let's have a cup of tea and get ourselves ready for living alone again." He came in, lifted me up, swung me around, and said, "Okay, Baby Girl, let's get going. Maybe she'll come back someday."

Toward the end of the summer, we decided to go upriver into the Nabesna area near Slana and find a good place to build a trapper's cabin. We started early one day, accompanied by five half-grown pups and seven pack dogs. The dogs carried all of our grub, cooking things, and bedding. Two days later, we turned from the windswept foothills of Mount Sanford to find a good site for the cabin at timberline. Our procession filed across a swampy flat that lay parallel to a heavily wooded creek.

As I glanced downcountry through tangled willow and scrawny spruce, I caught sight of a dark object on the flat beyond. I pointed to it and whispered, "There's a bear," and the outfit jerked to attention.

Slim whirled around to me and quietly asked, "Where?" I pointed again, and all ears and eyes were at full alert. The rattle of frying pans and chains ceased with the tense interest of the dogs. We could see the bear through the bush, and Slim said, "That's a black bear feeding on blueberries – just a harmless black bear. His coat would make a fine mattress for a camp bed, and it would be meat for the dogs." There was no question about it, we could use that bear.

Even the reddish nose that marks the black bear seemed plain at the distance he was from us, so we decided that I would take the high-powered rifle and get him. Slim would hold the dogs quiet and also control the pups. By making my way carefully through the creek thicket, I gained the upper end of the clear field where the bear was feeding. Between us was one stunted, tiny spruce tree. Its shelter was meager, but it gave me a lean for the rifle.

After judging the distance to be about six hundred yards, I sighted, aimed, and fired at the bear's broadside. There was no response, and so I fired again. He looked up, then fell, rolled over, and thrashed about, pawing the air. I watched him with that flash of pride, or triumph, or whatever you feel when, with a single encounter, you get meat, bed, and game.

Suddenly the bear leaped to his feet, and I fired again as he lumbered into the scraggly spruce forest. My bear was gone! Disappointed, I relaxed and started to reload the rifle. While pressing shells into the magazine, I glanced again at the berry patch I thought was empty, but it was not vacant. Through the scattered trees came a huge bundle of fury – the charging bear, and he was not black! He was a great hurling bulk of dark brown, a "silvertip." His reputation always meant trouble, and a wounded charging brown silvertip was a terror. With head down, limbs crisscrossing, and fur waving, he gathered momentum with every bound of gallop in my direction.

I pulled up the rifle and shot once, but it was too high. He was covering about three hundred yards in split seconds. I whirled and ran in leaps, screaming as loud as I could. I still remember exactly how the berry bushes and moss felt under my flying feet.

Oh, what a welcome sight and sound when Slim and the dogs with their clanking packs came over the bank of the creek in skirmish formation. With the arrival of an army of dogs, the bear veered into the brush of the creek.

He must have run a long way from us after the scare we had given him. (I can understand how he must have felt.)

After that experience we were more cautious in determining the color of a bear before we had any dealings with him. Certainly I shall never forget how that ordinary black bear, viewed at several hundred yards closer, turned into a deep-coated, magnificent silvertip on the rampage.

Well, we didn't have a black bearskin, but we still had me. After I sat down and shivered and shook for a few minutes, we continued on. We found a perfect spot for another cabin, and over the next few days, we built it. Our trip back to home base was less exciting. Days were getting colder, and winter was making itself felt.

Every passing season in Alaska added to my growing respect for the nature of the North. Its topography and weather defined its unique identity. Its environment seemed to be a force for proving the skill and endurance of its inhabitants. Whenever a man disappeared in the woods, died from exposure, or perished in the river, the explanation was, "The North got him." The many ruthless combinations of the Arctic sub-zero temperatures and the glacial streams were the most formidable, contriving ways to trap the unwary, or at least to add peril to their adventures.

The Copper River was no exception. It was a conniving body of water and frost. By November, ice was forming daily along its banks. Water was freezing to form shore-ice until it extended far into the river. Channel water, pressed from both sides, flowed smooth and high in its trough of ice. On the surface of the stream, slush-ice floes drifted that were as beautiful and as intricate as lace doilies. Particles of ice not larger than kernels of corn

Aileen at the Copper River cabin

adhered to each other in loose masses of varying breadth and depth. In their cohesion and their underwater thickness lay deadly danger. This I learned in a near fatal battle with the cloying stuff. Under these conditions, Slim and I had reason to cross the Copper River one day. Our regular rowboat was being repaired, so we fashioned a boat by covering a frame of alder poles with canvas, and chopped other poles into two crude oars. This makeshift craft was sturdy enough for several crossings of the slow-moving channel, which was perhaps sixty feet wide. We had made crafts like this many times and found them river-worthy, so we were not worried.

Standing at the edge of the shore-ice, we watched the congealing crystals of ice slide along. One moment the channel would be filled from bank to bank with the icy masses that were from ten to a hundred feet long, then there would be shorter open breaks. We waited for one of these breaks, being poised "on the mark, ready, set," as if for a dash across the street during heavy traffic. As a longer space of clear water swirled at our feet, we quickly launched our craft and took our places in it. Yet before the crude oars could be used to determine our position and direction, the current swung the boat about, and that delay cost us our crossing and nearly cost us our lives. Slush-ice cushions overtook the boat and clung to its canvas surface more tenaciously than they clove to one another. While the water had a cold of its own, canvas offered the greater cold of the atmosphere, so water began freezing fast to it.

Just two yards from solid shore we were caught, enmeshed in a gelid pudding of building ice. One of the oars became heavily weighted and was forcefully dragged away. The other we used as a paddle to scrape and push away at the growing frosty mush that seemed to have a will of its own. The boat grew more unwieldy as slush-ice built out from its sides and bottom. We were still six feet from shore and traveling downstream very fast.

Had I not been so busily engaged in paddling slush ice with my bare hands, I might have become frantic. Fear argued for expression through every fiber of my being. Self-preservation, however, kept me pressing and pushing at the congesting particles. The frail boat could not bear much more weight. Clear water a yard away was no help, for we could make no headway even toward the shore. Our efforts seemed useless. Moving one handful of slush only made space for more from below. To quit the boat would be no solution to our predicament, as the water was at least ten feet deep. The ice defied any attempt to swim, for it would entomb us.

Ahead of us, at a bend where the channel swung to the right, the ice floes crowded against the left bank. We worked even more furiously toward that milling mass in the eddy close to the shore. Our almost frenzied clawing at the top gave no perceptible assistance to the spewing action of the pent-up force underneath. Our boat was pulled about in the twisting mixture. The nose of the craft was shoved near anchored ice. When the gap closed we lost no seconds in jumping to safety. As we turned to rescue the boat, it was tipped, crumpled, and engulfed by sparkling medallions of slush-ice. Seconds later it slipped to an icy grave, never to be seen again. We had barely made it.

Walking back to our cabin, I felt wobbly from exertion and weak from fear and relief. We had added to our experience with the country. We had come through another close encounter with that forceful entity – the North.

Our mail piled up at Gakona while the river took its time freezing enough for us to get across. Our first trip down to get the mail and to break a trail was welcome. There was a big mail sack full of letters, magazines, and packages, and we could hardly wait to get home to open it.

That winter we had a dog team and a sled for us both. We broke many, many miles of snow and ice trail together, sometimes with Slim and his team in the lead and at other times with my outfit ahead. Rarely did we have to employ snowshoes for breaking a trail, with as many dogs as we had in line. We drove twelve dogs in all; usually Slim drove seven and I drove five. My sled was much smaller than his, but while I was much smaller than Slim, I hauled my share of the load nonetheless.

For the days when we had to stay in, we still dreamed of and planned a trip to Canada and maybe the States. It would probably take two winters of snow-trail mushing, with time out along the way to trap and replenish our finances. We would spend the summer on some clearwater stream. There we could find fish, game, and timber for cabin building, and perhaps find suitable soil for a small garden.

Then we turned to the most important requirement, other than our own willingness and preparedness for the undertaking – dogs. We needed dogs, strong dogs, excellent dogs, and plenty of them. To us, that meant dogs of wolf blood. The ones we had were not strong enough to endure the rigors of the planned adventure. In the meantime, Hoppy, our wolf, was growing into a huge and beautiful animal. Our hopes were still on him, but so far he had shown no interest in mating.

The trapping season was an adventure, as usual. We used both the Nabesna cabin and the Caribou Creek cabin. We had a good year, but we still wanted half-wolf pups.

After trapping season was over, we received a most unusual invitation.

Chief Stikwan of Copper Center was holding a potlatch. Only a few outside the tribal domain were ever allowed to be present, and we were invited. There were to be three non-Native guests: my husband, Slim Williams, who was a good friend of the Chief's; Florence "Ma" Barnes, the owner of Copper Center Roadhouse; and me, Aileen Gallaher Williams. It was indeed an honor, and we were excited about the event.

The potlatch is the outstanding social function of the Natives in the Copper River Valley. It signifies the end of mourning for an important member of one's family. For this one, the wife of the Chief was the important family member being mourned. It was to be held in the spring following her funeral. The river ice was still safe for dog team travel, and many could attend. The bereaved husband celebrated by giving away all his worldly possessions. Relatives and friends from near and far received guns, dogs, sleds, skins, moccasins, snowshoes, dried salmon, white-man canned goods – all the wealth accumulated by the host.

The things the man reserves for himself to start with again can cause a scandal, if he retains enough to appear comfortable against the elements and rigors of living off the land. A very wealthy Native will send messages of invitation to potlatch givers of the past, over a hundred-mile area. Such celebrations are reported by the guests, "Hiyu good potlatch—four days we sit-down that place."

Our host was not the richest man of the Copper Center Valley. He only had about seventy-five guests on the third and last evening of his potlatch. Most of the gifts had been distributed, and the singing and dancing was in progress when we presented ourselves with Ma Barnes at the doorway of Chief Stikwan's twenty-by-thirteen-foot frame shack.

Merry-making was at its height as the door was opened for our entrance. How space for our three chairs was found in that jam of people is a mystery. The walls were lined several deep with standing, squatting, or sitting Natives. In a clearance smaller than the proverbial nightclub dance floor, ten or more men of various ages and sizes milled, stomped, jumped, and twirled in individual expressions of traditional and fashionable Native dancing. All present participated in the chanting, the hand clapping, and the stomping. One young man was especially agile, outdoing the others with original steps and perspiration. Smoke, sweat, and very stale clothing held back the clean air outside a half-opened window. Sibilant whispers, giggles, and unchecked staring among those close about us, particularly women and girls, marked us as objects of discussion. Knowing some of their ways, I simply stared back.

The feast of stewed caribou and moose, rice, rotted-salmon-head delicacies, canned fruit, and strong black tea had been most successful. The fish delicacy, several hours later, was still adding its pungent aroma to the atmosphere.

Finally the host, excited by his wonderful party, dug deeper into his cache to further divest himself, and brought out a few last gifts. Among them was a pair of elaborately beaded, brand new moccasins of a very large size. To my amazement the object of this presentation was my husband. He was honored as an old friend, a "hiyu skookum" hunter, trapper, and fisher.

After about an hour's visit, we considered it polite to depart. The press of crowded bodies and clouded air assisted in our courteous decision. We thanked our host for an excellent evening and left the overcrowded shack.

The potlatch was a social achievement. The rich man had made his donations, properly distributing his wealth to the benefit of many relatives, family friends, and influential acquaintances. Chief Stikwan was proud of his generosity, and therefore happy. He had accomplished something that would long be remembered. His potlatch would be talked about until a bigger and better one would eclipse it. He could begin again to amass a fortune of guns, traps, sled, dogs, and skins, toward a time when death would take another family member worthy of a potlatch.

As we left the party, all three of us expressed our great honor and pleasure in having been invited. I had the wonderful feeling of belonging to the community and the marvelous land in which I lived.

WOLF PUPS

*L*ife was changing for Slim and me. I had ordered some pretty clothes from the Sears, Roebuck catalog, and Slim had some new togs too. After a good trapping season, we felt like having some social activity, so we visited all of our neighbors in the Copper River Valley. There were always more women in our community in the summer, so we had parties and dances. I enjoyed it all for a while, but one unpleasant part was Slim's apparent jealousy. When I danced with someone else, he would just stand and watch every move my partner and I made. We had been around other people so seldom that, until now, I had been unaware of his possessiveness. Nothing was ever said between us about it, but this spoiled our little ef-

Slim and Brandt

fort at social activity. I was eager to get back to our secluded little cabin on the river and see my wolf and dogs. Anyway, basically I was a loner, and home was where I was most happy. Conversation with one or two people was attractive, but a crowd never did appeal to me. So after an effort at social life, we went home.

How can I explain what happened to me when I saw my wolf? It was as though I would fill up with love for him until I thought I would burst. Slim did not understand this feeling, and again showed jealousy. I realized that as long as we were alone with no other men around, life with him was very good – except, of course, for Hoppy. I tried to subdue my feeling for the wolf as much as possible when Slim was near.

It had not been that way when we first got the wolf. Slim had been intensely interested in him, watching this animal with the same fascination as I had. Hoppy and I were very good with each other. I felt a love for him as I had never felt for any other pet. However, it seemed that as my feelings for the wolf increased, Slim's interest in him decreased.

That winter we started training Brandt for the lead. I never saw a dog in the North that could lift his head so high, step so high, and look so smooth from muzzle to tail tip. You expected to see dainty hooves instead of paws, the way he stepped and danced. He had lines, speed, vim, pride, alertness, and an eagerness to obey all orders. Brandt soon proved to us that he was a dog who reasoned, and that kind of dog earns the status of leader.

We wanted to have pups with Hoppy as the father, but the wolf did not seem very eager to mate with our females. He was about three years old that fall. Two of our best females were in heat, but he didn't show any interest. So I took Stub into Hoppy's circle and chained her there. She actually seduced that wolf, and when the mating took place, we were overjoyed. Then I took Klute and chained her to Hoppy. It was also successful, because now he knew what to do.

After the mating, Hoppy was a different animal. All the groveling and crouching was gone. He acted as though he were head of the pack, although he remained loving and affectionate to me. We eagerly awaited the arrival of his offspring, our first half-wolf pups.

We expected the great event in the spring. Due to the extreme cold during that April, we made beds for Stub and Klute in the cabin. One was in Samme's former bedroom and the other was in what could be called the living room. At that time of year there would not be company, and we were thrilled to give cabin space to such an important event. As the time grew near, I sat up into the small hours of the night awaiting the arrival of the first litter.

There is something that I have pondered for years. Several times I have been with mother dogs, both domestic and part wolf, and I was welcome, even missed, by the mothers if I was not closely attentive. But the presence of Slim, or any other man, was not encouraged, and some mothers even growled at him threateningly. I later found that the dogs of wolf-mixture were more apt to growl.

I comforted Klute as she dropped ten half-wolf pups. As they dried off, I could see that there were only three light-colored ones. I was a bit disappointed, because I preferred the tan-gray of the timber wolf. Hoppy was yellow, and I wanted more than three to look like him.

Soon Stub also began her ordeal and dropped five puppies. I am sure that dear little Stub felt a bit bothered that she only had five, for she was very eager to take two orphaned, full-dog pups which were born the same time as the others. Their mother, Goldie, had an unplanned mating with Sonki, and she would have nothing to do with them. We also gave two of Klute's babies to Stub. This gave her nine pups to mother, and made her happy.

Stub's half-wolf pups, four black and one gray, grew to be leggy, eary, and taily monsters with swinging gaits and steps that were almost leaps. After they were weaned we sold all but five of Klute's puppies, then in due time we named the rest. Slim named Spike when he was about two months old, because his ears were the first to stand up rigidly. I named the four females. Gypsy was so named because I simply liked the name for a female. Copper was named for the river and valley, and Ginger for her color. Wrangell, my dear and loving yellow girl, I named for Mount Wrangell. Like her father, Hoppy, Wrangell and I were close, with a deep affinity for each other.

We watched with fascination and enjoyment as the wolf pups grew. I actually neglected housework at times to watch them playing, sleeping, and going to "school" with their father, Hoppy. The way he treated his own pups was remarkably different from his treatment of the dog pups. He knew his offspring, put them through rigid training, and gave them tender loving. He would chew and maul and snap at their tiny bodies with fangs covered by lips. They learned how to charge for the throat, crunch the forepaws, and rip at the abdomen. Hoppy plainly taught them many things, not only the defensive and offensive in fighting and playing, but the game of tug-of-war, how to cache excess food, and how to get away from insects by digging a cave. I think he taught them chorus work also, because I had seen him start a solo and encourage them to join him. The dogs would just sit and look either puzzled or amused, I could never tell which. He would also regurgitate his food for his own pups.

Once, at about midnight, we found Hoppy almost standing on his head trying to reach a porcupine, which had carelessly walked in among the dog kennels. Hoppy was doing this very quietly until suddenly the dogs got wind of the intruder and there was an excited uproar. This caused the porcupine to move into Hoppy's reach. Oh, yes! I pulled three quills out of his nose, and a fourth, which had broken short in his jaw. This wild, wild wolf of all the fables allowed me to remove the quill from his jaw without a murmur. He had the intelligence to know what was needed, and my love for him made me unafraid.

Hoppy and one of his sons

We had many visitors who were interested in seeing Hoppy and his pups. The wolf's reaction to a person – stranger or friend, man or woman – would always be immediately apparent. Some were entirely ignored, while others would have their finger sniffed or licked, or would perhaps even be honored by being allowed to pet him. Why the difference? Ask your dog.

Sensitive as he was, Hoppy still didn't travel well, so that summer we again left him at our main cabin in the care of a neighbor. We were crossing the bare mountain from Sheep Creek to a building site about sixty miles from the Copper River cabin. Our dogs, each carrying supplies, followed along obediently, and the five half-wolf pups ran loose but always stayed close to their pack. Suddenly when we got to the top of a small hill, we saw a large herd of caribou in a meadow below us. We thought the half-wolf pups would most certainly desert us at the first glimpse or scent of the herd, but no! They just looked, trotted to the next small knoll, and watched the caribou gallop and leap away. However, we had to contain the pack dogs by chaining them together in two bunches, restraining them so they would not take off after the caribou. If we had not contained these dogs, they would have run wildly after the caribou and carried off our bed and rations, which their canvas packs held. The wolf pups, however, seemed to know instinctively that it was fruitless to chase wildly after a whole herd of caribou.

Eventually the pups were big and strong enough to carry packs. They proved to be much better packers than the pure dogs. They were longer-legged, which was to their advantage in carrying a pack. They were also much more sensitive to surrounding conditions like jutting logs, detaining brush, branches, and uprooted stumps. Sensing these objects, they would either turn back to find a clearer opening, or crouch, or leap to avoid catching ropes or packs. A dog will get tangled up and helplessly bark at falling behind, or blunder through an obstacle, tearing the pack and ripping it open. Hoppy must have whispered many hints to his "kids," for they did not wind up and tangle when chained to a tree, as a dog will. I never saw Hoppy get the least bit tangled up, something I've seen many a dog accomplish.

When sledding time arrived that fall, we put one or two of the half-wolves at a time into harness, and took short trips of trail breaking. They did remarkably well. Only one seemed out of order. Ginger never learned that she was safe and should be calm. She always tensed with fear, shied, wouldn't stand, and had a horror of the sled no matter how we coaxed and explained. When a man wanted her for a brood animal, we let him have her. That left us four of Hoppy's pups – Spike, Wrangell, Copper, and Gypsy. The dogs of the team were Brandt, Beaver, Pat, Buck, and Klute.

Alone one day with nine dogs and a loaded sled, I decided to test a new leader. Wrangell had shown signs of leadership, so I decided to try her out. I called, "Whoa," and the team stopped and looked around to see what I wanted at this stretch in the river, where there was neither trap nor ice nor dangerous trail. Through crusty snow fifteen inches deep, I waded to the lead dog, Beaver, and changed places with him and the new leader. He seemed unhappy to give up his place.

When Wrangell was snapped into the lead position, she turned about to mill among the dogs. I thought, Oh, bother, and yelled, "Mush, Wrangell, mush!" In a flash she turned and leaped into place at a gallop, the excited team at her heels. It was a split second movement, and there I stood in heavy snow. As the sled slid by me, I jumped to catch it, and found myself holding the top of the sled and dragging. Unable to get my feet under me fast enough or strongly enough, I could not get on the sled runners where I belonged. The team dashed on. I called out to "whoa," but they were too excited to obey. They had a new leader to chase and she didn't look back.

When my arms began to weaken, I gripped the sled only nine inches from the snow. This left me dragging along full length. The trail, smooth under the sled runners, was not firm or smooth in the center. It appeared even, but snaking along on the stomach at ten miles an

Hoppy's half wolf pups

hour made every clot of snow feel like a stone shot into my flesh. I begged the dogs to stop. I cursed and demanded, but it did no good. It was one of their disobedient dashes. As we went into a curve I could see my new leader forty-five feet ahead. She paid no attention to my demands.

I could not resign myself to letting the team go. Even if they did reach home without injuring one or two dogs, I risked my reputation. A dog-musher who lost her team? Never! I took several more yards of beating. Finally I could endure no more. Better to let go while I might still be able to walk. When I did, the sled leaped away from me. Gasping for air, I climbed to my feet. With what seemed like the last effort I would ever make, I ran after the team.

In a sharp turn, the sled nosed into the deep snow and the rascals slowed down. I was able to catch up, and when I did, I got up on the sled runners and collapsed forward onto the load. Dazed and groggy, I whispered

for them to pull away, snowdrift and all. In a few minutes I was able to get the load onto the trail. The dogs,
still excited over their new leader, fairly sailed home.
Oh, how I clung to that sled! Slim was a little reluctant
to believe my story until, by chance, a trapper reported
my escapade as he saw it written in the snow. For a
half-mile I had been thumped in the solar plexus, but
the rule of the North, "never lose your dogteam," had
not been broken.

It was 1930, the trapping season was over, and with
spring approaching we decided to move. The Copper River
cabin was old when Slim moved into it, and we wanted to
be free of always having to row across the river to get to
the car. Slim had at one time lived at Sourdough on the
Gulkana River, and thought it might be a good place to
start. We rented a little cabin on the river behind the old
Roadhouse. It was no small task to move our outfit, but
our friend Tommy Hyke eased the undertaking with his
truck.

The fun of finding a site for the cabin we wanted to
build occupied our days. We discovered a beautiful spot
about two miles upriver from Sourdough. The land was
higher than the surrounding area, and the river flowed
directly to it and turned. Our cabin would be facing the
river with a freshwater stream on the right side. It would
be the largest cabin we would build, and we planned to
start in the early fall.

In the meantime, we received a letter from Samme.
She wanted to come back to Alaska and us. Slim said, "I
told you. I knew she'd come back." Our return letter to
her contained the ticket for the SS *Aleutian*, leaving August 16 from Seattle and arriving in Valdez on August 21.

We would be there to meet her. We didn't tell her that she was going to help build another cabin.

It was a happy day for us when my dear sister hurried down the gangplank and into our arms again.

PART IV

Samme Gallaher

1930-1931

MY RETURN

*I*t had been two years since I left Aileen and Slim standing on the dock at Valdez, and the memory of my year with them had never been far from my thoughts. Returning to school had been fun. I was frequently called upon to tell about my adventures in Alaska, and I became a celebrity at Fresno High. However, as I was reading a book about Alaska, the descriptions of rivers, mountains, ice, snow, and dog teams filled me with a yearning to be in that land. I tried to rid myself of the feeling, but it would not go away, and I longed to go back. Remembering the joy of living there with Aileen and Slim – the fun of driving a dog team, the beauty of the river and trees – overwhelmed me, and I knew I had to return. It would put

Samme at the airport on her return trip to Alaska, 1931

me back another year in school, but that had not been a problem before. Going to Alaska for another year would not really harm my education but only delay it. After talking it over with my parents, they agreed to let me go, if Aileen and Slim wanted me to return. Mother and my sister Una drove me to the San Francisco Bay Airdrome, and I flew to Seattle in a Fokker F-10-A Trimotor Monoplane. In 1930 West Coast Air was one of the first scheduled airlines in the world. It took us many hours to fly eight hundred miles to Seattle, and we had to land in a field for refueling. The service man pumped gasoline from a huge barrel with a hand pump, but all went well. That evening, from the Atwater Hotel in Seattle, I phoned mother and spoke to her for the last time for a year. The next morning I boarded the *SS Aleutian* at the Alaska Steamship dock, and I was on my way to Alaska again.

It was truly a memorable journey. On board was a group of men who were going on an extended hunting trip into Alaska's Interior. When they heard that I had lived in the Copper River Valley, and that a girl my age had shot caribou and driven a dog team, they were amazed. Also, I was acquainted with one of their guides, Harry Boyden. They were all interested in my adventures, and asked me many questions about my life in the wilderness. Two of these men were very well known – General Robert E. Wood, the president of Sears, Roebuck and Co., and Wendell Endicott, director – and they became my new friends. General Wood was interested when I told him that we bought most of our clothing and household goods from the Sears catalog. He wanted me to select something from the catalog that he could send me when he returned to Chicago, but I was shy about doing so. He said that I had been so generous in telling my adventures he wanted to show his gratitude. He and another member of his party, Mr. Perry, selected a radio for me. Mr. Endicott gave me his autographed book about an earlier Alaska hunting trip. They left the ship at Cordova, but Harry Boyden came back for a visit with me while the ship was in dock there. Later I wrote to thank General Wood for the radio, and we began a correspondence that lasted many years. He was the most gracious gentleman I have ever known.

When the ship docked in Valdez, Aileen and Slim were waiting for me with open arms. Oh, it was so good to be back! We had so much to say to each other that we were all talking at once. Finally we quieted down a little, and they told me there was a surprise in store for me. It turned out to be an airplane ride to Copper Center.

Bush pilot Harold Gillam and Sertza, a Siberian sled dog

Aileen and I had the big thrill of flying to the Interior with bush pilot Harold Gillam in his little open cockpit airplane. It was a rare sunny day for Valdez, and we were able to see sheep on the side of the mountain. We flew right over the Worthington Glacier with the mountains towering above us on both sides. Then as we left the mountains, we dropped down into the Copper River Valley and could see the river winding its way to the ocean. Above it stood the great mountain sentinels of the valley: Blackburn, Wrangell, Drum, and Sanford. What a beautiful sight on a clear day! In a little over an hour after takeoff, Gillam landed the craft at the little Copper Center airstrip, a journey that in the gold rush days took weeks of hard work to accomplish.

Slim drove the car from Valdez and met us at Copper Center two hours or so later, and we joined him for the rest of our trip home.

When we arrived at the little house at Sourdough, I was surprised. I didn't know they had moved, but it didn't matter, because the dogs and Hoppy were there. Also, there were a few I hadn't met, the half-wolf dogs. Aileen introduced me to Wrangell, Copper, Gypsy, and Spike. What a bunch of lovers they were! As I petted them, they rolled over, whined, and let out little fountains of pee. They were very emotional. The other dogs greeted me in such a way that made me believe they remembered me. I just can't put into words how it felt to be back with those big, beautiful creatures. Aileen and Slim just watched the greeting, loving that was going on. Finally they went in the house and soon I followed, bursting into tears. I was a bit emotional too, but I had more control than the dogs.

After my flood of tears was over, we laughed at my silliness. Then they told me about the cabin that I was going to help build. The next day we got into our hiking clothes and walked up to the cabin site. It was a beautiful spot about ten feet higher than the Gulkana River, which flowed directly toward the site and then turned in front. A little creek tumbled down the bank on the right side, and there was a pool where it flowed into the river, which appeared to be a great place to fish.

I looked around and noticed the area had no trees for building. I asked Slim, "What are we going to use for logs?"

They both laughed and Aileen said, "That's why we need you. Follow us." We walked upriver for about a quarter of a mile, and there was a beautiful stand of trees, straight, tall, and all about the same size.

"How do we get them to the cabin site?" I asked.

Pointing to the river, Slim answered, "We float them down, and then hoist them up the bank." Well, that sounded like a big job to me, and that is exactly what it turned out to be.

The rest of the summer, we did a lot of visiting, and
we were often at the Gakona Roadhouse, as it was still
our mailing address. On one occasion, there were a number of people sitting around talking when a tall, dirty,
thin man walked in. We all watched him, and then someone said, "That's Donald MacDonald, the highway engi-
neer, who has just returned from one of his long survey-
ing missions, and he is usually gone for weeks at a time."
He went to a chair, sat down, and took off his boots. Then
he very carefully took off one sock. He dropped it on the
floor and it just stood up by itself. He watched it intently
and after a few seconds, the sock began to crumple down.
Mr. MacDonald shook his head and said, "Darn, I haven't
been out long enough."

In September we started work on the new cabin. Slim
pitched a tent for us to live in while we did the building
and installed a Yukon stove. We outlined the floor plan
of the cabin as our first project. We then got our axes in
hand and started for the trees. Slim would cut down a
tree and then cut off the top branches, making a sort of
runway for Aileen and me to walk along the top of the
log and chop off the side branches. Then Slim cleaned
the branches off the bottom and measured and cut the
log to size. Each log had to be individually floated down
the river to a little beach in front of the site. To get them
up the bank, Slim made a windlass and stood it next to the
floor plan. To the windlass he attached two ropes with
loops at each end. He would put these around the end of
the log, and with a heavy pole under the log, he would
hoist it up about a foot. Aileen and I worked the windlass
to help raise the log and hold it in place. This procedure
was repeated until the log finally reached the top.

The finished cabin measured fifteen by twenty feet, and each log went through the same process. Slim did all of the notching and fitting, and Aileen and I helped move the logs into place. We also did all of the chinking between the logs we could reach with moss and mud, and Slim did the rest. We started in September, and it took us until early December to finish. It was a beautiful log cabin home, facing the Gulkana River, and we were quite proud of our achievement.

In front of the cabin, there was a big tree stump where I loved to stand and sing. I would sing to the river, to the birds, to the dogs, and to myself. In the pool that our little stream made as it joined the big river, Aileen and I would fly-fish. In a very short time, we could fill a tub with enough whitefish and grayling to feed all of the dogs and ourselves. What a heavenly spot we had!

One evening we witnessed a very strange thing. The full moon was at about the ten o'clock position in the sky, and we suddenly saw a bright light moving northward at a moderately fast speed. As it passed in front of the moon, it became a dark object. Then it turned to the bright light again until it was out of sight. It was no airplane, as lights that bright and big were not yet installed on aircraft. It was just a big mystery we never solved, and we were the only ones who saw it.

We returned to the Caribou Creek cabin for the trapping season that winter, and it was a particularly hard trip. We traveled on the Copper River ice to the mouth of the creek and camped there for the night. For our beds we dug a deep hole in a snowbank, wrapped up in a blanket, and snuggled down to sleep. It was New Year's Eve, and for fireworks that night, we had all the

Samme and Aileen at the Gulkana River, 1930

bright stars of heaven. Instead of noisemakers, the dogs and the wolf started howling about midnight. That was how we welcomed in the year of 1931.

We had expected easy going up the creek. However, the ice was not solid and the sled kept breaking through onto rocks, so we had to travel alongside the creek bed. This was rough going, as the snow was very deep. Twice we had to stop, make some tea, and give the dogs and ourselves a rest. We cached some of our load as the ravine narrowed and the snow got deeper. Then, finally we had to tie Hoppy to a tree. He was not in the team as a worker but tied so he could run beside the dogs. In the extremely deep snow, he was having a hard time keeping up. We hated to leave him, but we didn't have any choice. The minute we left, he started howling in the dark. It was eerie.

The drifts were so deep that when I took a step, I'd fall through to my thigh. The labor of walking was exhausting. We cached the rest of the load. Slim went ahead on snowshoes to make a trail for the dogs, but it didn't help much. Aileen was manning the sled, which was also a hard job. The snow was so dry it wouldn't pack, and the dogs had a rough time pulling even an empty sled through it. We finally arrived at the cabin, and I went to sleep standing up. It took us twenty-four hours to cover twelve miles, including the rest stops.

The next day Aileen and Slim went back down the trail we had broken to retrieve Hoppy from his lonely tree, and was he happy to get back to his family after a night in the woods.

I was happy, too. I found the little cabin I had helped build two years before the same as I remembered. It seemed hard to believe that I was there again. This year our team was a lot stronger and Slim was able to cover more ground on the trap line. Aileen would go with him one day, and I would go the next. Whoever stayed home did the cooking, and Hoppy was there to talk to and pet. He was always so loving and responsive to any attention given him. I came to love him almost as much as Aileen did.

The days that I spent at the cabin alone were valuable to me because the solitude changed me. Being there in the vast wilderness gave me a sense of the enormity of the universe, and it humbled me. I became more aware of my own identity, and of a feeling of strength within me. I know that I grew up quite a bit that winter.

The days passed by much too quickly, and when the trapping season was over, we headed for home to Gulkana. The trip down the creek was much easier because we had made a trail on our hard journey up.

We arrived home tired but happy. Still, there was much work to be done in connection with the trapping. Furs had to be put on drying racks and fleshed. Slim did most of that, as he knew how. Then, after the pelts were finished, he took them to the fur buyers. When he returned, we all rejoiced, because it had been a good season.

Life was very simple those days. Because there was a lot of wind and bad weather, we mostly stayed home. Aileen would read serials to us from the *Saturday Evening Post*. We especially enjoyed "Mutiny on the Bounty." I did the cooking, and Slim sat and rolled his own cigarettes. When Slim shot a goose, I had the pleasure of plucking it, and it was very good eating, as we had not had meat for some time. Finally Slim said, "I am going

*Aileen and Samme helped build this cabin
on the Gulkana River.*

to go hunting and get a moose." He left about ten o'clock
and came back at three o'clock with a moose liver. Even
with the dogs' help, it took quite a while to bring in the
rest of the welcome meat.

Then, on the second of March, one moment shat-
tered our peace and changed our lives. Aileen had a
migraine headache that day, which caused her to be
irritable. Slim got the camera, and for some reason he
wanted a picture of Aileen with Hoppy. She told him
that she didn't feel well enough to have a picture taken,
but he became very insistent, which was not like him.
Finally she gave in and said, "Oh, all right, but don't
take too long." She went out to the wolf without check-
ing his mood. When she walked into his circle and
squatted down, Hoppy came over to her and put his

face right up to hers. Slim took a couple of pictures.
When she abruptly stood up, Hoppy playfully lunged
at her and nipped her near the waist. It surprised her,
and she cried out. He did not pierce her skin, but just
sort of pinched her. Thinking nothing of it, she and I
went into the house but as we sat down, there was a
rifle shot. Aileen looked at me and said, "Hoppy!"
Then she groaned, fainted, and slid out of her chair to
the floor. In tears, I knelt frantically beside her and
tried to bring her to. Slim came in. Alarmed to see her
on the floor, he tried to rouse her, but she was out for
what seemed a very long time. When she finally opened
her eyes, they were dull. She sat up and appeared completely lost. I helped her to her feet, and we slowly
walked into her room, where she stretched out across
the bed. I went to my room and put my pillow over my
head so they would not hear me sobbing. Aileen did
not utter one word until the next day.

I don't believe Aileen ever cried over Hoppy, but I'm
sure she never forgave Slim. She knew Hoppy had only
been playing. She had seen him play with his pups and
bite them with covered teeth. If he were vicious, he could
have ripped her open.

Aileen was heartsick. She never mentioned Hoppy
in any way, but her sense of joy was gone. She only
spoke to Slim when it was necessary, and she would not
look right at me, because she seemed to know that if she
did, I would start to cry. It was as though she had lost
contact with existence. Over time, however, she gradually became more normal, and the tension lessened.

Finally Aileen decided to get away from the Gulkana
home for a while, so later that spring and summer we

moved down to a small rented house at Copper Center. It was at the end of the airstrip and Harold Gillam, the pilot, was our constant visitor. There was much social activity, and one of Aileen's high school friends, Theo Crozier, came up for a visit. Aileen, Gillam, and I drove into Valdez to meet her ship. There were two interesting young men, Albert Rafn and Seton Thompson, who were at our house almost every evening. They were ichthyologists studying the migration and spawning of the salmon. We had a lot of company and fun.

From the air, Harold Gillam had discovered a strange lake not very far from Copper Center. He wanted to hike over there to see it, so we got together a group that was interested in the adventure: Aileen, Slim, Theo, Gillam, Seton, Alfred, and me. It was a whole day's outing, and we took Beaver along to pack our lunch. The lake looked like a crater and was very salty. It killed all the vegetation below where it drained. No one, to our knowledge, had ever seen it before and it was not on any map. We called it "Mystery Lake."

Our lunch of ham sandwiches on Aileen's homemade bread had to be eaten standing up. There was no place to sit down around the edge of the lake. We were all thirsty, as we could not drink the lake water. Slim scouted around until he finally found a freshwater stream feeding into the lake. Seton was busy with his camera and I with mine. Gillam seemed very pleased with his discovery.

During this time at Copper Center there were many dances and social events. We hosted one big day when almost the whole population of Copper Center came out to our place for a shoot. We set up targets in a field

*Shooting match at Copper Center, 1931. Harold Gillam, Al Rafn
(behind post), Slim Williams, Indian children, Seton Thompson*

and had a contest to see who could hit the bull's-eye
the most times. Aileen was the best shot in the whole
crowd.

I was nineteen by then, and I thought I was in love
with Gillam. All the ladies liked him, because he was a
charming man and rather romantic. He had a new rub-
ber raft that he wanted to try out, and he asked me to go
with him. I was really thrilled at the attention he gave
me while we floated down the Copper River for a couple
of miles. Of course he was not interested in me, but he
was interested in someone else in our group – my sister,
Aileen. She said nothing to me about how she felt toward him, but I began to notice that she would light up

when he was around. I knew of Slim's jealous posses-siveness of her, and wondered if he noticed.

One night at a dance, "all hell" broke loose. Aileen and Gillam were dancing and everyone was watching them, because by now, the attraction they had for each other was becoming noticeable. Perhaps they were dancing a little too close, because Slim suddenly became angry, walked over to them, and asked Gillam to step outside. The fight that took place was bloody. Slim really beat up on Gillam, in spite of several men who tried to stop him. Finally a group managed to end the fight. Well, you can imagine what happened to that party. We went home, and the at-mosphere was grim.

It was several days before we began to resume some normal conversation, and the only thing we talked about was my trip home. I know it was very hard for Aileen to let me go. The mood in our cabin had greatly chilled since the day Huppy was killed, and now after that fight, it was frigid.

When it was time for me to go, we drove to Valdez, where I boarded the ship. Aileen and Slim stood on the dock the same way they had done two years ago. They both waved as the ship pulled away, and stood there a long time.

In Seattle, Gillam's mother and sister met me when the ship docked and the next day took me to the train. It was good to be going home to my family, but I was wor-ried about Aileen and Slim in the cabin on the Gulkana River.

PART V

Aileen Gallaher

1931-1933

THE BROKEN TRAIL

*T*he day we said goodbye to Samme was an unhappy time for me. There was not very much to talk about on our drive home from Valdez. We parked the car, and said nothing on the walk up the river from Sourdough to our cabin. Since Hoppy was gone, it was almost unbearable for me to return. The dogs greeted us as usual, but for me the ache of not seeing my wolf was almost intolerable. Now, with Samme gone, I felt a deep sorrow that had to be controlled. It was like being on a tough trail with miles to go, and you just have to keep going. As we went into the house, I turned to Slim and said, "We need to talk." He nodded his head in agreement.

Slim wanted to know about my feelings for Gillam. He asked me if I loved him, and I answered, "I think so. I have never had this feeling for anyone else in my life. But what made you so angry as to beat him up? There was no reason to do that. We had not even held hands, and the dancing was as close as we had ever been to each other. You know I have always cared for you, but now, after you've killed Hoppy and fought with Gillam, I feel as though I don't know you, and I don't know what to do."

He took my hand and after a few moments, said, "Aileen, I know you haven't loved me as I've loved you, and I've been jealous of anything or anyone that you did love. I always resented Hoppy because you loved him so much, and when I noticed your feelings for Gillam, I just lost my head. I don't believe you've ever understood how I feel about you. I was a lonesome man living alone in the woods, and you – a beautiful young woman – were eager and willing to share my life. I knew the possibility of failure in our relationship was high, but after a few months, I felt that we would succeed. You seemed to be happy with me and I felt proud that you were mine. I was the only man in the area who had a companion like you – young, strong, and beautiful – and I was ready to fight for you."

When I started to cry then, he reached out, put his arm around me, and said, "We can never be less than friends, so what do we do now?"

I pulled away from him and answered, "Let's not do anything, and just try to go on as before." And that's what we did, except that I moved into Samme's room, and we worked and lived together as pals from then on.

As summer faded into fall, we took a vacation, and Tommy Hyke came to take care of our home and feed the dogs. Our drive to Fairbanks up the Richardson High-

Aileen Gallaher Williams, 1932

way was an adventure. The road was rough, and we
forded a few little creeks. In Fairbanks we met some
friends and went to the mountains to hunt sheep. I was
lucky, as I was the only one who killed a sheep that day.
We enjoyed our trip, and when we returned home our
life became somewhat normal again.

We still talked about the long journey we could make. Slim decided that if we did, we would need a better sled than we now used, so we built another one. It was a strong one made to withstand the pressure and beating of a rough trap-line trail, and it was a most unusual sled. The timber came from the States, and the steel runners were special, being wider and sturdier than most. At twenty-six inches wide and nine feet long, it was the widest sled in the valley. Men would stare at it and study it because of its size. The brake, which had been made in a Kennecott Mine blacksmith shop, was welded steel.

Many times that winter I shoved that sled over a trail. I cursed and sweated when it became unruly with a load and slid off the hard-packed trail. Once when that massive brake didn't completely hold in the snow, my dogs almost tangled with a Native and his team. I had a terrific struggle to dissuade Beaver and Pat from their intention to charge into the other team. Standing on the brake as hard as I could, I cracked the whip over their heads and yelled at them to get back on the trail. They reluctantly obeyed then, and the other team went around us. It was one of my many close calls.

In early January, Wrangell and Gypsy were expecting quarter-wolf pups. Pat and Brandt were the fathers. We were trapping at Caribou Creek that winter, and the cabin was too small for the event, so we built a small log cabin next to ours. We chinked the logs with what we could find in sub-zero weather – some moss, newspaper and magazine paper, sawdust, and gunnysacks. Then we packed snow on the roof and sides. Never were there better quarters for expectant mother dogs north of sixty-two degrees.

Gypsy had six pups and Wrangell had seven, and I was once again busy and happy. How we guarded and cared for those pups! When they were about a week old, we placed those thirteen quarter-wolf pups on the bunk in our cabin. I studied and fondled them, and I can still see each one vividly, as I saw them that morning.

Near the end of trapping season, the pups were about six weeks old and could be left alone. Slim made a little pen to keep them from wandering away from their kennel, which enabled me to go with him to help on the trap line.

The first day that I went with Slim was like most other days on the low slope of Mount Sanford. We had been out since daylight and had made the rounds of our traps. There were a few good pelts in our sled, and we headed home. The dogs were a bit sluggish and seemed a bit weary after a day's work. It was close to sundown and would start to get dark early, as there was a slight overcast.

Slim was manning the sled, and I was coming along in the rear. He stopped the dogs and said, "I just have to take a leak. It's been a long day." So I just turned around and looked back at the mountain. It could have been the last time I would ever see it, because just as Slim adjusted his clothes, the dogs took off in a dash. Slim yelled for them to "whoa," but he got no response. He immediately started after the team and shouted for me to go on home.

After recovering from the shock of being out there all alone with no dogs or man or gun, I started on down the trail to the cabin. There were about two more miles to go, and it was getting dark. I could just barely see

Slim with sled

the trail. A couple of times I got off into the deeper snow but managed to feel my way back to the harder area of the trail. By this time, it was dark with only the faintest bit of twilight. I knew that by now I should be dropping down to the creek, but to my anguish, I realized that I was gradually climbing. I had lost the path completely and was going directly opposite to the way home. Panic began to well up in me. I knew

that a night on Mount Sanford at twenty or more below zero would be my last.

Through the darkness, I could hardly see what looked
like a darker area, and I made my way over to it. It was a
scrub pine, and it gave me a ray of hope. If I could start a
fire, Slim would see it, as I knew he would be out there
someplace looking for me. I tried my best to get some
small branches, but I couldn't reach them. It had already
been a long day before those damn dogs had bolted, and
I was exhausted and frightened. True desperation took
hold of me, but I knew that I must try not to let it control
me. A wind had come up, however, and I could now feel
the cold even more acutely. In despair, I slumped down
in the snow and put my hands up over my face as though
to blot out my plight.

Suddenly I heard six rapid-fire shots from a long way
off. Then, after as long as it takes to reload a rifle, there
were six more shots. I knew that Slim was out there someplace, signaling me. Staggering to my feet, I started in
the direction from which the shots came. Gradually I
could hear the sound of the sled and Slim calling me, and
then I could barely see him and the dogs through the darkness.

My voice was so weak he couldn't hear me when I
called out. There was no strength left in my legs to run to
him through the deep snow. I watched him passing by
as though he were a shadow in the dark, and felt as if my
life was going with him. All at once, he stopped, turned
the team in my direction, and then he saw me! When he
reached me, he picked me up, put me in the sled, and
took off his parka to cover me, as I was shivering from
cold and fear.

"It was Klute who heard you. Her ears went up, she looked and pulled to the left, and when I turned and peered through the darkness, I could just make you out. Thank God for Klute, she saved your life," Slim said.

When we got home, Slim told me that he'd had a hard time catching the dogs. He believed that they had seen some caribou and started after them. When he caught up with the team, they had turned the sled over, which slowed them down. He then turned them around and went to the cabin. He expected me to be there by then, and alarmed when I was not, he immediately went back up the trail to find me. It had been about three hours since the dogs had run away. Believe me, three hours groping through the snow at twenty below in the dark on the slope of Mount Sanford is an experience no one would ever want to repeat.

Trapping season ended, and we started home with all the pelts we had collected and those wonderful quarter-wolf puppies. What a time we had on the trail keeping everything in order! Wrangell and Copper were still nursing their babies, and we would have to stop for the procedure. If we hadn't made that big sled, we would have had to make two trips. I was relieved when we finally pulled into the yard of the Gulkana River cabin, but my heart ached again, without Hoppy to greet us.

I turned my attention to the other precious dogs, and tried to forget and forgive. The joy of having a yard full of pups took most of my time. I knew that when they were old enough, most of them would have to be sold. We finally sold all but four. The ones we kept were Baldy, Trompis, Wrinklebrow, and Frosty. When they were old enough to start early training, I spent most of my time with them, but the old ache over Hoppy would not go away.

On the surface, our life seemed all right, but deep down, it was not. I still resented the fact that Slim had killed Hoppy, and I kept remembering that bloody fight he had with Gillam. We hadn't seen or heard from Gillam since that night.

Then there grew a strange yearning within me that I could not define. At first I thought it was spring fever, and then I realized I was homesick. I was heart-broken over Hoppy and Gillam, and I wanted to go home to my mother in Fresno, California. Slim agreed, with resignation, probably understanding more than I wanted him to.

Now, thinking of my departure, I realized that I hadn't been out of the woods for six years. It would be a shock, but how much? A few hours before I left the cabin, I went out to bid farewell to the dogs – my dear team. I whispered, "I'll be seeing you sometime," and tears came that I could not control. As I left the yard, the dogs were all on their feet, watching, waving at me with tails, and dancing their attention. It was the twenty-fifth of June, 1932, when we got into the car to drive to Valdez. Before I boarded the ship, I cried again as Slim held me in his arms. He understood my sorrow at leaving and my need for going. He kissed me goodbye and whispered, "I'll miss you."

The voyage down the Inside Passage was beautiful, and I began to get that wonderful feeling of going home. I was eager to see my mother and the rest of the family. When we landed in Seattle and went ashore, I found what years of Northern silence could do to a person. The noise of the city throbbed and pounded through me. I couldn't hear or think, and I felt like a bundle of steel knots. Every step on pavement was a hammer blow up my spine that seemed to lodge in my head. It gradually began to ease off, and I found myself amazed at seeing changes I had only heard about.

When I visited with my relatives in Portland, Oregon, on the way home, they seemed too forward, too affectionate and free with each other. I felt embarrassed, even affronted by their attention, as though I were being pursued. When I analyzed my feelings about them, I realized how reticent I had become during those six years of solitude with Slim. I simply needed to get accustomed to being with other people again. My reunion with my dear mother and family in Fresno was wonderful. I relished the intense heat of the San Joaquin Valley as I never had before. And I loved seeing and hearing the movies! The talkies were exciting, and it was sometimes amusing to hear the voices of my former matinee idols.

While I was doing these things, Slim wrote that he was moving up the Copper River to build yet another cabin. The pups were breaking fine, there had even been a light fall of snow in September. The freeze-up had come, and many other things that had forecast the swift arrival of winter and another trapping season.

I had become acquainted with Slim's people – several sisters, nieces, nephews, and a brother. They rarely heard from Slim. Then one day in November, one of his sisters called me on the telephone. She was excited and asked me if I had seen a certain San Francisco newspaper about a man from Alaska who was to travel by dogsled to Chicago for the World's Fair. I told her I had not. She read to me a short notice on the front page and asked me if that was Slim. I said, "Oh, yes, there is no question about it being Slim." The dateline of Cordova, the starting point at Copper Center, the description of the man, the team, and the destination all proved it to be "our" trip. I verified this to his sister and to others who inquired.

Filled with joy and pride at the undertaking, I was also almost sick with disappointment. I wanted to be there with Slim and the dogs, venturing into magnificent wild country on an unbroken trail to an unprecedented goal for a dog team. Several men had attempted the trip with dogs before, but never made it farther than a few hundred miles.

The dogs in the team he was driving were brothers Brandt and Pat; Wrangell, Gypsy, and Copper (Hoppy's offspring); and Baldy, Trompis, Wrinklebrow, and Frosty (the quarter wolves). My Hoppy was well represented in that long journey. They were all so dear to me, as I had been with their mothers when they were born.

Since I had first heard of the trip from a newspaper, I waited anxiously for a letter. Four days later, I received word from Slim. He said that there was no fur in the country, no caribou, and he had nothing to do but travel, so it may as well be to the States. The next day I received a wire that he sent as he left the Copper River Valley, and later a letter that had been written at the same time arrived by mail. Then came long weeks with no word at all.

About the middle of December I prepared a lengthy telegram, which included messages from some of his folks and mine. The clerk in the telegraph office first thought that Dawson was in Alaska, and it took some persuasion to convince him Canada was the right location.

When Slim got to Dawson, he had our Christmas telegram and a special honor awaiting him. The Highway Association of Alaska and Yukon, with headquarters in Fairbanks and Dawson, had elected him as official Trail Blazer of the proposed highway. Besides a life membership card in the Association, he was given aid with charts, and directions for his itinerary, which he sent to me in a letter.

If Slim's trip down through Canada and across the States would promote a highway to Alaska, what a triumph that would be! Then many more people would be able to travel to the North and see the beauty of Alaska.

Before he left Dawson for Whitehorse on Christmas day, he sent a wire. I knew he would get some good trail at that time of year, for there would be some kind of sled travel by that time, and all ice should be firm and safe by January. In spite of this, I still waited anxiously for the next news of his journey.

From my comfortable chair in sunny California, I could mentally travel many miles of the way with him. I could summon the picture of a good trail and calm weather, and know the speed he was making. I could mentally fight into a blizzard, break trail through frigid misery, make open camp in darkness, and explore overflow water and slush atop river or lake. I could do all this, and bring Slim and those precious, courageous dogs through, by pitting their combined strength against Lady North. I remembered the unexpected turns, the sudden hazards, and the lightning changes of the ever-strange conditions in the North and the woods. Although I felt certain all through the trip that they would make it, I suffered many terrors on the mental trail I covered with them.

It had been almost five months since Slim had started the journey, and as he was nearing the States, he wrote to me and asked me to join him in Spokane, Washington. Slim's brother Freeman, and his wife and daughter, Patricia, were driving up from Fresno, and he wanted me to come with them.

We drove up to Spokane and met him there. It was good seeing him and the dogs again. He had replaced the sled runners with wheels, as there was no snow on the ground. We would drive ahead of him, scouting and securing camps for all of us and the dogs. We were in civilized country and couldn't just camp wherever we wanted. I traveled with them for six weeks as Slim crossed Idaho and Montana, but then I became ill and had to return to Fresno.

Slim continued to his destination, the World's Fair in Chicago. There, in a special exhibit, he showed his dog team and sled and shared information about his journey. He caught the attention of First Lady Eleanor Roosevelt, who told reporters that she thought he and his dogs were the most interesting thing at the event. After the Fair closed, Slim continued on to Washington, D.C., where he visited the White House and met President Roosevelt.

After Slim and the dogs had their adventure in Chicago and Washington, D.C., they returned to Fresno where he stayed with his sister at her ranch. I went out now and then to see Slim and the dogs. We talked about our marriage and realized it was over. He had found someone on his travels who was interested in him. I was happy for him and we parted. I never saw the dogs or Slim again.

It was a long time before I could bring myself to talk about my wolf, the dogs, and my adventures in Alaska. As I sit here many years later, I can still imagine a stand of lovely birch trees on a flat, dry stretch of land. The spring snow is well packed, forming a solid trail for the dogs and sled. Suddenly the dogs pick up a scent – maybe a caribou, a moose, or even an Indian camp – and leap into a reckless race. I hold tight to the sled with hands and feet and I feel as though I am flying, and should something go wrong, the sled break or collide with a log, I would fly! For at least a half-mile, the dogs gallop at full speed, their tails out straight, feet flinging snow particles as far back as the sled end, where I am clutching for my balance. The dogs finally slow down, panting with their tongues hanging out, happy for the chase.

With all the comfort of my city life, is it surprising that I have moments of longing for the North woods? I don't know what that primitive kind of life did to me, but whatever it was, it remains to this day. I have moments when my memory of some particular spot – the bank of a certain stream near a group of spruce trees, a yellow smelly swamp meadow, or just our trail, cutting its way along the three great mountains – becomes more real in my mind than today's news. Maybe other places exist that can do that to a person. I don't know, but I would not trade my Alaska experience for any other.

EPILOGUE

The beauty of Alaska captivated me, and I will always cherish the six years I spent there. Slim was such a good partner, and for most of those years, we had a happy life together. However, the parting of the ways came, and it all ended. There were times that I missed him very much. I kept in touch with his sister and heard about his activities.

He remarried in Chicago soon after the divorce. Then later, in 1939, Slim was back in the press with yet another publicity stunt to promote a highway to Alaska, this time with motorcycles. He and a young partner, John Logan, traveled from Fairbanks to Vancouver, BC It was the first time that trip had been made with motorized vehicles.

Fri-Nov- 3, 1933

Mrs. Roosevelt Praises Feat Of Fresnans' Kin

Loved His Dogs

CLYDE C. (SLIM) WILLIAMS

Praises of the First Lady today were heaped upon C. C. Williams of Alaska, son-in-law of Mrs. Blanche Gallaher of Fresno, for his unique feat of driving a team of Alaskan huskies 4,600 miles to the world's fair in Chicago.

None other than Mrs. Franklin D. Roosevelt, wife of the president, told newswriters at her press conference at the White House that what she liked best about the Chicago exposition "was the man who drove the huskies down all the way from Alaska."

It was high praise for Williams, who made the long dogsled trek to promote an international highway to Alaska. Mrs. Roosevelt said she had "a perfectly grand time."

"The driver has the kind of blue eyes that look away off to distant horizons," said Mrs. Roosevelt. "I loved his dogs. They were grand. I was careful of them and polite to them and asked if I might pat them. There were two, only half wolf, that it was all right for me to pat."

With the closing of the world's fair, Williams, a brother-in-law of Mrs. W. R. Jolley of Fresno, plans to go to Washington to see President Roosevelt in behalf of the proposed highway.

Slim also took city children on short trips into the Alaska wilderness, teaching them survival. A book was published about him that was more fiction than fact. He lectured about Alaska for many years with a scheduled lecture tour company. Slim survived to the age of ninety-three, passing away in 1974.

In 1957 I went to Alaska with my mother, Blanche, and it was one of the most enjoyable trips of our lives. She had the pleasure of sailing up the Inside Passage; then we went to where I had lived, and I showed her the beauty of the woods and the rivers.

We gazed upon those sentinels of the Copper River Valley, Mount Wrangell, Mount Drum, and Mount Sanford, forever in my heart and soul. The adventures beneath those mountains in that valley will be with me always.

PART VI

Afterword

AFTERWORD

*A*ileen adjusted well to life in Fresno after she returned from Alaska in 1932. She was interested in all of the changes that had occurred the six years she was gone. Eager to continue her education, she went back to high school, graduated, and attended Fresno State College for a couple of years where she excelled as a student. It was there that she wrote about her life and adventures in Alaska, material that finds its way into this book almost eighty years after the fact.

Eventually Aileen went to Hollywood and was attached to a studio to help direct dog team sequences. But she did not like what she encountered in Tinseltown and came back to Fresno.

There she married Julius Hansen, the lawyer who
helped her obtain her divorce from Slim, and settled down
to small-town life, working as legal secretary for her husband. During this period they took two boat trips to Alaska,
but she did not return to the Copper River Valley.

∞

In 1952 Aileen divorced her second husband and
moved to San Rafael, California, living there with our
mother, who had been widowed in 1934 when Dad died
of an appendicitis attack. Nearby was our sister Una, who
had settled down to marry David Reed Lawrence and
raise their daughter, Geraldine.

With Mother for company, Aileen finally returned to
the Copper River Valley in 1957. The only person she saw
there from her past was Tommy Hyke, who was still driving his truck and helping people. But when our mother
saw the magnificent mountains and the glacial streams,
she finally understood her daughters' fascination for
Alaska.

In the late 1950s, Ike Bailey, the mechanic who was
Aileen's steady beau before she met Slim Williams, looked
her up. He had visited Mother occasionally over the years
that Aileen was gone, and never lost touch. Now he was
in the last stages of a divorce, and he and Aileen picked
up the pieces of their earlier romance. Aileen found him
to be the most wonderful kind of man she had ever
dreamed of. They were to be married as soon as his divorce was final, but Ike died unexpectedly from a cere-
bral hemorrhage. Aileen eventually recovered, but she
would not be happy until later on when she and I were
together again.

∞

My life after my return from Alaska is another book. After graduating from high school, I went to Fresno State College and then married an artist. Four years with him was almost four years too many. After divorcing him, I, too, went to Hollywood where I studied voice and acting and sang in many opera vignettes. But like my sister Aileen, I realized Hollywood was not for me and returned to Fresno.

There I worked for North American Aviation where I met a wonderful red-headed pilot, Carl Von Darnall. We were married three weeks later, and I found myself the stepmother of Clark, a nine-year-old handful.

Soon after, we went to live in Glasgow, Montana, on the northeastern prairie, where we opened an airplane business that included aerial crop spraying. Carl taught me how to fly a Piper Cub, but I didn't do any of the crop spraying. That was left to the experts.

After eight years in Montana, we moved to Friday Harbor in the San Juan Islands where we bought a thirty-two-foot boat and converted it into a gillnetter and fished at night on the Salmon Banks in Puget Sound. We also commuted in season to run our crop spraying business in Montana, and prospered.

Aileen and Mother built a custom log house near us in Friday Harbor, and it was a dream come true for us to be together. However, after mother had a slight stroke, she and Aileen returned to San Rafael to be with our sister. My husband's health began to fail. He had smoked since he was thirteen and died of lung cancer in 1967. My mother passed away just three months later.

In an attempt to recover, Aileen and I took a number of trips abroad including a cruise up the Norwegian coast. But nothing we saw compared to the beauty of the Inside Passage to Alaska. We still missed that country terribly, but at first we could not talk about it without undo emotion. Finally we were able to live it again in memory. How we had loved the freedom, the beauty, the dogs, Slim, and Hoppy, our big wolf!

Aileen had what I called long-distance vision. She could see caribou that neither Slim nor I could until we were much closer to them. So it was devastating to us when her sight began to fail. Six months before her death in 1994 she was completely blind. But she was beautiful to the end with practically no wrinkles and little sign of aging.   I believe she had removed herself emotionally from this life and lived her wilderness experience. I would sometimes see her with a longing expression on her face, and if I asked what she was thinking, she would just look at me and smile. She died peacefully just a few days before her eighty-ninth birthday.

My stepson, Clark Darnall, turned out very well indeed. After a successful career in Army Intelligence, he graduated from University of Washington as an oceanographer and went on to become renowned in his field in many lands. When he died in 1997, the Norwegian government flew its flags at half-mast for a day and floated part of his ashes on the sea.

∞

What became of the other Alaskans who were once so much a part of our lives in what we both counted among our happiest days?

After two seasons at the Chicago Fair and a visit to the White House, Slim Williams came back to Fresno, shipping the dogs to his sister's ranch there. Aileen and I went out to see the animals, and there was much whining and petting. They were so happy to see her again. She had helped raise and train them, and they had been a big part of her life. Some of them I'd come to love as pups. Yet when we walked away, we knew that we would never see them again.

After Aileen and Slim decided on a divorce, Slim returned to Chicago where he met Gladys Pennington whom he wed in 1936. Three years later, he and John Logan made a trip from Alaska to Seattle on motorcycles.

Gladys became Slim's manager, and during the next few years, he earned his living by lecturing about Alaska, making the most of his beautiful deep voice and his special way of spinning a yarn. He was a great promoter of Alaska and the idea of an international highway to the Far North, which he would see realized with the building of the Alcan Highway during World War II.

Slim also took two groups of young boys on adventure trips to Alaska. Then he finally retired to the Chicago area to spend most of his time writing. He died in 1974 at the age of 93. Bob King, the historian who wrote the introduction to this book, is currently working on Williams biography.

∞

Today, on the lawn in front of the Gakona Roadhouse stands on old, rusted wagon, the one on which I rode with Arne Sundt up the frozen Copper River in the winter of 1927 just before he sought my hand in marriage from Slim, my horrified guardian. And it was a good thing for Arne that Slim said, "No." On a trip to his home-land, Norway, Sundt met a lovely girl named Henra Lehn who, in 1932, made the long journey from Norway to Alaska alone. When she arrived in Cordova, Arne was there, waiting for her. They were married at the home of Ben and Andine Osborne, Arne's Norwegian friends, and settled in Gakona. Henra adjusted well to Alaska and they had three children. I believe it is safe to say that Arne and Henra started the first family of the Copper River Valley who were not Natives.

For some years, Arne and his partner, John Paulsen, operated the Slate Creek Mining Company. When the gold ran out in the mine, Arne spent his time running the Gakona Lodge and being a father to his sons, Arne and Ronald, and his daughter, Marguerite. But in 1946, Arne died unexpectedly from a heart attack, which was a dread-ful loss to the little family

Henra continued to run the business at Gakona, but during most of this time, she was separated from her chil-dren because there was no educational system in the val-ley and they had to be sent away to school. Finally, after thirty years, she sold the lodge and moved to Anchorage where her children had settled. She died in the summer of 2002 at age ninety-four.

∞

I never saw John Meggett, the romance of my early years, after we waved goodbye on the dock in Juneau in 1928. We corresponded for more than a year, but when I returned in 1930, he didn't know that I had come back to Alaska. Later I learned he had graduated from the Uni-versity of Alaska in Fairbanks with a degree in civil engineering and teaching. He served as an Army captain in World War II, married, and had two sons.

In 1986 I found his name in the telephone book for Bellingham, Washington, where he had retired. We had an animated conversation, happy to have caught up after all the years, but that was the last time I talked to him. I was living nearby in Vashon, Washington, at the time, but was in the process of moving back to California. In 2002 his family informed me that he had passed on.

∞

Although Aileen was in love with Harold Gillam, and Gillam's parents were kind enough to meet me at the Seattle dock when I landed there alone in 1931, neither of us ever saw the handsome flyer again after leaving Alaska.

The unknown was a challenge to this man, and he was hard to read. No one called him Harold. We all used his surname. I'm sure that he slept, like any human being, but I never saw him when he was tired or sleepy. Gillam was mainly interested in his flying. He did little talking about any of his trips, which included a daring rescue mission to Siberia. He also made a second wild foray there where Russians gave him a little white, curly haired sled dog named Sertza that Aileen took care of whenever he was gone.

Gillam took chances that no one else would, and could find his way in storms and darkness. When he was not flying, he was busy working on his craft. In 1931 we rented a little house from John McCrary in Copper Center, and we saw Gillam almost every day. He was a good listener but quiet, and he never talked about his personal life. He was called a ladies' man because women loved him. He was a romantic figure, not handsome by movie standards but charming and interesting. He took this adoration of the opposite sex in his stride, never seeming to notice it. One young woman that summer actually followed him around. He did not pay too much attention to her but was always kind. Finally it became known that he had a wife and son in Fairbanks, but he did not live there. We thought it was strange that he never mentioned his son, but that was his personal business.

When the pilot lost his life in a plane crash in 1943, Aileen and I were deeply saddened. He had been, we recalled, the only visitor we ever had that our pet wolf allowed near him. Gillam was a wonderful, unusual man, and we were proud to have known and loved him.

∞

Red Hurst, our friend who ran the roadhouse at Chistochina and drove his Ford down the ice-laden Copper River in winter to get supplies, had been attacked by a ferocious grizzly bear. With one swipe of his enormous claws, the bear scalped Red along one side of his head. The men with him pushed the torn scalp back into place, bandaged Red up with his shirt, and stopped the bleeding. The kind of medical help Red needed for his injury was not available in Alaska, so he went to Seattle and spent a few weeks in the hospital.

After he was released, Red stayed at the Atwood Hotel, but he found the din of the city almost painful and was afraid to cross the streets. He never told us how he got back. He did say that when his hair grew back it was redder than ever.

Red had helped build the roadhouse there in Chistochina in 1922, and as long as I knew him, he was always there. He was a good cook, and you could always count on a tasty meal at his table. The last I heard of Red, he had finally moved from Chistochina, had married a Native woman, and lived up in the Nabesna area.

∽

Florence Barnes, who owned the Copper Center Roadhouse, had came from New Zealand to Alaska after she had gone through a dreadful epidemic. She was a nurse and had worked day and night caring for the sick. For fear of contaminaton, people slept rolled up in blankets on the hillside. When she got through with that experience, she vowed to find a new life and she found it in Copper Center, Alaska. The roadhouse there was for sale and she bought it.

When I met her for the first time at age fifteen, she treated me like an adult. She directed her attention and interest to me whenever I conversed with her. Ma was that way with everyone.

We often stayed overnight at the roadhouse, and every evening Pan (Panganie, a card game that was highly popular with pioneering Alaskans) was played in the dining room. After supper, the big table would be cleared and the game would start. It was fascinating to watch Ma deal. The players would call for cards, and if they wanted four, she would rapidly deal three cards on the table in front of her and with the fourth card swoop up the other cards and toss them to the player. Each time, they would plop down right in front of him, even though he might be at the other end of the table. I never saw her miss or fumble the deck. I don't know who won the game or what they won, because I had to go to bed and Pan was played all night.

Ma Barnes ran the roadhouse for many years, and it was the center of much of the activity of Copper Center. There is one account where she closed the bar on the Fourth of July and the community had a glorious sober celebration.

Finally, the right man finally came along. George Livingstone was age seventy and she was sixty-nine when they decided to be married there in Copper Center. However, George heard that some Road Commission men planned a big party for them, so they decided to go to the states for the ceremony. They got as far as Victoria, B.C., when Ma became ill and died from a heart attack. Mr. Livingstone brought her back to Copper Center for the funeral.

Ma's death was a great loss to Copper Center, and an even greater for Lucy Craig, Ma's little girl. When Lucy was five years old, her father Charles Craig died leaving his Native wife with four children across the river from Ma's roadhouse with no solid means of support. Ma was very concerned about them and took Lucy under her wing because she was the youngest and most needful. The child lived with Ma during the summer, and in the fall, she was sent outside to the Indian School at Salem, Oregon.

Ma kept her well clothed and made her silk underwear from her own petticoat. When Lucy showed off her silk panties to one of the boarders and he said, "They are so lovely and I hope you will always wear silk." In a way, she always did.

After Lucy graduated from high school in Portland, Oregon, she married

Alton Smithart, a Navy man. They had four children— Charles, John, Audrey and Gloria. Then, after much water had flown under Lucy's bridge, she married Leonard Brenwick, an Alaska man from Kennicott. They built a business at Klutina on the Copper Center Loop and operated it for many years.

When Lucy's brother and husband built the road the locals called Craig-Brenwick, she went to Juneau to secure the name of the road, telling government officials that there were too many things being named for people who had never been in Alaska, like Mount McKinley. She got the petition, and the name for the road was secured. After Mr. Brenwick died, Lucy sold the business and built a home in Copper Center.

When I was reunited with Lucy in 2001, we had no prior knowledge of each other's whereabouts. A friend, Doug Vollman, saw her picture with the wolf in my album, and asked who she was. I told him that it was a girl named Lucy Craig, whom I had met in 1927. He said that he knew of only one person like that in the valley and she was called Lucille.

"Let's call her and find out," I suggested. She was not home, so I left a message that said, "If you are the Lucy that knew Aileen and Slim Williams and Samme Gallaher who lived on the Copper River, please call back." In a few minutes the phone rang and an excited voice said, "I'm that Lucy."

I renewed my friendship with Lucille in Copper Center to discover she was just as full of vim and vigor as she was when we were fifteen years old. One thing about this

Reunion of Lucy and Samme in 2001

little lady, she never sauntered anywhere in her life. It was always full speed ahead.

I visited her again the next year, too. We had fun and enjoyed our time together. But when I said goodbye, she took my hand and held it for a few moments.

"I wonder if we will ever see each other again," she said. Two months later, the day after the big earthquake, she died at age ninety-one.

∞

In 2000 I returned to Alaska with my niece Geri, her husband, Earle, and their son, Jeff. We rode the ferry system to Juneau and then took another ferry to Valdez, where we rented a car and drove to the Copper River Valley.

We took a rafting trip down the Copper River and found the ruins of the cabin where I had lived in 1927. It was dilapidated and out of use, but when I saw that old cast-iron cooking stove, I said, "Oh, there's Aileen's old stove" and burst out crying.

It was very emotional for me to be there again. I don't think I have recovered yet, but I've enjoyed going back every year since. Like my sister, Aileen, a part of my heart remains forever in the great land we both loved, the Copper River Valley.

Copper River

RECOMMENDATIONS FOR READERS
INTERESTED IN ALASKA BOOKS BY AND ABOUT WOMEN

ACCIDENTAL ADVENTURER:
Memoir of the First Woman to Climb Mt. McKinley,
by Barbara Washburn, trade paperback, $16.95

COLD RIVER SPIRITS:
The Legacy of an Athabascan-Irish family from Alaska's Yukon River,
by Jan Harper-Haines, hardbound, $19.95

FLY FISHING WOMEN EXPLORE ALASKA,
by Cecilia "Pudge" Kleinkauf, trade paperback, $19.95

IDITAROD DREAMS:
A Year in the Life of Sled Dog Racer DeeDee Jonrowe,
by Lew Freedman, trade paperback, $14.95

GO FOR IT!
Finding Your Own Frontier
Judith Kleinfeld, Ed.D., trade paperback, $14.95

GOOD TIME GIRLS OF THE ALASKA-YUKON GOLD RUSH,
by Lael Morgan, trade paperback, $17.95

RAISING OURSELVES:
A Gwitch'in Coming of Age Story from the Yukon River,
by Velma Wallis, trade paperback, $14.95

SEVEN WORDS FOR WIND:
Essays and Field Notes from Alaska's Pribilof Islands,
by Sumner MacLeish, hardbound edition, $17.95.

These titles can be found at or special-ordered from your local bookstore. These and other Alaska books also can be ordered directly from the publisher by calling 1-800-950-6663, or by visiting EpicenterPress.com or writing to Epicenter Press, P.O. Box 82368, Kenmore, WA 98028. Visa, MC accepted. Add $4.95 s/h for one book, $6.95 for two or more. WA residents add 8.7% sales tax.